Information Technology Management
Evolving Managerial Roles

Howard O. Rockness
School of Business Administration
University of North Carolina

Robert W. Zmud
College of Business
Florida State University

A Publication of
Financial Executives Research Foundation

Financial Executives Research Foundation
10 Madison Avenue, P.O. Box 1938
Morristown, New Jersey 07962-1938

International Standard Book Number 0-910586-71-3
Library of Congress Catalog Card Number 89-80587
Printed in the United States of America
First Printing

Financial Executives Research Foundation is the research affiliate of Financial
Executives Institute. The basic purpose of the Foundation is to conduct research and
publish informative material in the field of business management, with particular
emphasis on the practices of financial management and its evolving role in the
management of business.

The views set forth in this publication are those of the author(s) and do not
necessarily represent those of the FERF Board as a whole, individual trustees,
or the members of the Project Advisory Committee.

Information Technology Management
Evolving Managerial Roles

Acknowledgments

The authors wish to recognize the immense contributions of Andrew C. Boynton (University of Virginia) to the entire research project and the help of Angell Beza (University of North Carolina) in the development of the survey questionnaire.

About the Authors

HOWARD ROCKNESS is Associate Dean and Professor of Accounting, School of Business, University of North Carolina at Chapel Hill. He holds B.S.M.E., MBA, and PhD degrees, all from the University of Washington in Seattle, Washington. He teaches, consults, and does research in the areas of accounting, management control systems, and information systems.

ROBERT ZMUD is Professor and Thomas L. Williams, Jr., Eminent Scholar in Management Information Systems in the Information and Management Science Department at the College of Business, Florida State University. His current research interests focus on the impact of information technology in facilitating a variety of organizational behaviors and on organizational efforts involved with planning, managing, and diffusing information technology. Dr. Zmud has consulted with numerous organizations, has published extensively in both practitioner and scholarly journals, and has editorial responsibilities with a number of major journals in the information systems field.

Project Advisory Committee

John F. Dykes
Vice President–Finance
Emgraph, Inc.

Joseph H. Joiner
Vice-President (Retired)
Georgia Pacific Corporation

Carl E. Norman
Senior Vice President–Finance and CFO
CSX Resorts

Marshall N. Mortin
Vice President–Controller
West Point–Pepperell, Inc.

Herbert A. Philips (Chairman)
Senior Vice President
Equifax, Inc.

Donald Wood
Partner (Retired)
Touche Ross

Nancy K. Farlow
Publications Manager
Financial Executives Research Foundation

Contents

Part I
An Overview of the Study

1
Introduction and Executive Summary

The following six key trends significantly affect the way in which infomation technologies (IT) and information services (IS) are managed today:

1. Advances in technology continue to improve the capabilities and reduce the costs of IT while increasing both the size and complexity of an organization's IT investments.

2. Heightened awareness of the usefulness and potential of IT exists at all managerial levels.

3. Those activities most central to an organization's success in the marketplace are increasingly dependent on IT applications.

4. Growing demand for IT applications are exceeding the delivery capacity of corporate IS groups.

5. Acquisition of IT resources occurs more often via channels other than the corporate IS group.

6. Automated operating and network control systems offer increased sophistication and greater ease of use.

Taken together, these trends raise serious questions about how to best manage IT. More specifically, the key concern at issue is the following:

How can we direct and coordinate IS activities where appropriate without losing the advantages of line managers making IT decisions.

This study will provide solutions for this as well as other problems for corporate managers interested in managing their investment in IT more effectively.

The study focuses on five areas:

1. Providing a historical perspective for examining IT management issues.

2. Presenting summary data on a large group of companies (including their current IT environments).

3. Summarizing the IT decision-making environments found in these companies, including an analysis of who makes each of a wide variety of IT decisions.

4. Examining relationships in these companies regarding the location of IT decision making and (a) business unit performance, (b) business unit use of IT, and (c) IS/user relations.

5. Providing in-depth descriptions of how a carefully selected set of companies is applying IT, how they make IT decisions, and the factors they believe to be critical to successful IT implementation.

Data used to derive the study's findings are based on survey results obtained from chief financial officers (CFO), chief information officers (CIO), and business unit managers in 79 business units drawn from 35 companies as well as on case studies of eight of these companies.

Our interpretation of the findings of the research project produced two overall observations and six general guidelines for IT management.

Overall Observations

1. Most organizations today are in transition regarding the location of IT management responsibilities.

2. In this transition, responsibilities for a number of IS activities are moving from the corporate IS group to either divisional IS groups or to line management. Clearly, the organizational role of the corporate IS organization, and hence of the CIO, is being redefined.

General Guidelines

1. Moving responsibility for short-run IT decisions from corporate IS to business units is linked with higher performing business units.

2. The strategic use of IT requires the coordinated actions of corporate IS, divisional IS, and business unit line managers with regard to IT decision making.

3. Greater line involvement in IT decision making results in business units' performing better and exhibiting both a greater reliance on IT and higher quality IS/user relations.

4. Greater line manager involvement in IT decision making occurs when divisional IS directors report to their divisions' senior executive rather than their divisions' controller.

5. Locating decision responsibilities for IT project management and for IT operations within the divisional IS group is linked with higher business unit performance and a greater reliance on the use of IT to support business unit operations and strategies.

6. Invariably, better relations are observed between users and the divisional IS staff than between users and the corporate IS staff.

2
Evolving Patterns of Information Technology Management

It is well documented that information technology is drastically reshaping the way work is performed, the nature of organizations, and the functioning of markets.[1] Information technology includes the full spectrum of computational and telecommunication hardware and software applied by organizations to support their business operations. What is not as well recognized, nor understood, is that corresponding changes are occurring in the manner in which IT is being managed. Expressed simply, organizational responsibility for many information services activities is believed to be moving from the corporate IS group to divisional IS groups and line management. Here, IS activities encompass all management and technical efforts required to introduce and utilize IT.

Four Eras of IT Management

It is often overlooked that many business organizations have more than 100 years of experience managing information (in some form) and more than 30 years of experience in using and managing computer-based IT. Over these years, technological advances have transformed IT from a seemingly magical, expensive but limited piece of business equipment to an indispensable, affordable business and management tool used throughout most organizations. Today these technological advances are accelerating.

Major shifts in the way organizations manage IT also have occurred over this period of time. We have classified these shifts into four major eras of IT management: the "default" era, the "monopoly" era, the "business within a business" era, and the "information economy" era.

The 1950s: Default

Electronic computers often were used first by operational or low-level staff departments at the initiative of a knowledgable manager, engineer, or other professional who recognized the computer's potential for handling straightforward data processing tasks. Most often, management responsibility for IT "defaulted" to those individuals applying the technology. For example, Table 2.1 lists the initial organizational location of the information services unit in 45 business organizations.[2]

TABLE 2.1   **Initial Location of Corporate IS Group**

Location	Number
accounting	5
planning	2
production	3
controller	10
finance	10
administrative services	8
autonomous information services unit	7

In those early days of computing, very little application software and few computer professionals (e.g., programmers or analysts) were available. Managers, other business professionals, or their staffs wrote programs, entered data, operated equipment, and distributed output. As the number of computer applications within a department increased, formal job roles as programmers, analysts, computer operators, and computer managers appeared. Most often, though, the new positions reported to managers within the line or staff function where the computer was used.

The 1960s and early 1970s: A Monopoly

The benefits gained from automating a business's information flows led most organizations to integrate their core business applications throughout the 1960s. Because such integration efforts had to contend with limited systems software, nonstandardized applications software, and incompatible hardware, specialists skilled in a variety of hardware and software fields were required. The growing complexity of computing gave rise to a centralized, or corporate, IS group within which most, if not all, IT management responsibilities were handled.

This corporate IS group primarily served a *manufacturing* role by configuring and operating a production facility consisting of large-scale computer systems as well as by establishing and maintaining a sizable in-house application development group. Typically, this corporate IS group was organized with four subfunctions: operations, systems development, technical support, and administration. Table 2.2 lists those IS activities normally associated with each of these subfunctions. Because all computer-based information needs were funneled through it, the corporate IS group held a virtual monopoly on the organization's IS activities.

TABLE 2.2 **Traditional IT Management Activities**

Subfunction	Activities
operations	data preparation/entry
	data/information distribution
	input/output controls
	hardware acquisition
	hardware installation
	hardware operation/maintenance
	file storage/controls
	job scheduling
systems development	systems planning
	feasibility studies
	systems analysis/design
	application programming/testing
	package software acquisition
	systems conversions
	user training
	application maintenance
technical support	systems software acquisition
	systems software installation
	systems software maintenance
	communications (data) analysis/design
	communications (data) installation
	communications (data) maintenance
	communications (data) management
	database analysis/design
	database installation
	database conversions
	database management
administration	capacity planning
	budgeting
	systems personnel management
	systems personnel training
	standards development

Mid-1970s to mid-1980s: Business within a Business

The IT environment of most businesses changed significantly during this time period. Information technology was increasingly applied to support managers and professional staff and to extend core applications beyond the organization's boundaries. In addition, the proliferation of IT products and services from third-party suppliers (e.g., vendors for minicomputers, microcomputers, workstations, generic software packages for both business applications and personal support, external data services, etc.) created a dramatic shift in the nature of the activities of the corporate IS group. It was not until this era that the role played by IT in most organizations evolved from simply that of "data processing" to one truly representative of the term "information support."

While a *manufacturing* role was still important, two new roles emerged: a *distribution* role and a *technology transfer* role. The distribution role arose when organizations recognized the multiple channels through which IT products and services could be obtained. Application software, for example, could be acquired through an in-house software development group, through the use of end-user development tools, through the packaged software industry, through time-sharing services, or through a systems house. The technology transfer role has evolved from organized efforts to keep aware of, to experiment with, and to introduce new IT products and services. Many organizations, for example, established office automation (OA) or computer integrated manufacturing (CIM) groups to develop plans, policies, and support services to facilitate the diffusion of these technologies across work units. Table 2.3 provides an overview of the expanded set of activities now associated with IT management.[3]

The following are some of the numerous changes that occurred in the nature of IT management during this period of time:

— All IT (computers, voice and data communications, etc.) was located under a single authority.

— Information technology was recognized as a potentially important element of an organization's business strategies.

— Information technology resources were physically distributed to operating units throughout the organization.

— Third-party sourcing of IT resources greatly increased.

— The organizational level of the CIO rose.

— The corporate IS group began to view itself as a "service center."

Few substantive changes, however, were observed in the location of IT management responsibilities.

Late-1980s and on: Information Economy

Examination of many of today's organizations indicates that operating units are pulling IT resources both *physically* and *managerially* closer to themselves. Line

TABLE 2.3   **Expanded IT Management Activities**

Subfunction	Activities
delivery systems	operations activities (see Table 2.2) end-user facilities support end-user liason quality assurance database support communications (voice and data) support hardware maintenance systems software maintenance capacity planning develop and maintain the technological infrastructure
systems development	system design and software development for production systems, for critical systems, for sensitive systems, for corporate-wide systems, and for software tools
support center	internal consulting service for organizational analyses, decision modeling, feasibility studies, and systems analyses
information center	broker for packaged software, external data services, microcomputers, etc. end user and systems personnel training internal consulting and support facilities facilities for user developed applications
technology scanning	monitor technological developments technological forecasting examine potential of new technologies
technology transfer	plan and manage pilot studies plan and manage implementations of new technology plan and manage transfer of applications across work units
planning	liason with corporate strategic planning explore opportunities for strategic systems overall information planning evaluation of organization's IT usage establish IT standards and policies
quality assessment	security planning and standards evaluation of/adherence to standards
administration	budgeting systems personnel management document management

managers, staff professionals, and even senior managers are initiating and implementing IT applications, often in reaction to competitors' actions, sometimes in conjunction with and at other times independent of the corporate IS group. Expressed most simply, IT resources and IS activities are being dispersed throughout the organization.

This emerging IT environment might best be thought of as an *information economy within the business.*[4] In this economy, an "information business" is defined as any operating or work unit that produces a deliverable information product or service by applying IT resources that the unit itself owns and manages. Many managers and professionals outside of the corporate IS group are becoming increasingly skilled in applying technologies, such as CAD/CAM workstations, financial modeling software, database software, decision support software, and local area networks. Often, these business professionals are experts regarding specific technologies. With such expertise at their disposal, line and staff managers and professionals often are willing and able to identify IT opportunities and implement effective IT applications to pursue them.

Current Patterns in IT Managerial Responsibilities

Aside from prescriptions from experts, little has been reported about current patterns of IT managerial responsibilities.[5] Two articles, however, do provide some data on these patterns.

The first presents the results of a survey of CIOs in 20 leading-edge business organizations undertaken in 1983 by the MIT Center for Information Systems Research (CISR).[6] Table 2.4 indicates which activities were identified by a majority of respondents as the responsibility of either the corporate IS group, divisional or subsidiary IS groups, or line management.

Three major observations were made. First, a decentralization of IT development and operations activities is taking place. Most of these responsibilities, however, are being shifted to divisional IS groups. Second, the corporate IS group is playing a less dominant role in terms of its control of IT expenditures. On average, the corporate IS group controlled only 48 percent of IT expenditures in these firms. Third, the IT management responsibilities of the corporate IS group are increasingly staff- oriented, rather than line-oriented.

The second article provides a penetrating and comprehensive examination of a reorganization of IS activities at Manufacturers Hanover Corporation (MHC).[7] In April 1985, MHC announced a major reorganization into five business sectors in order to give each sector executive maximum control over all needed resources, including IT resources, and complete accountability for performance.

TABLE 2.4   **Results of CISR Study**

Corporate IS Activities:

   IS strategic planning
   technology scanning/anticipation
   mainframe/mini approval/standards
   telecommunications/voice approval/standards
   telecommunications/data approval/standards
   systems life cycle standards
   national/multinational vendor contracts
   security/privacy standards
   IS consulting services/technical expertise
   senior management education
   line users education
   executive support
   internal timesharing

Divisional IS Activities:

   multi-year and annual budgets
   multi-year and annual project plans
   applications architecture planning
   applications planning
   mainframe/mini operation
   personal computer selection
   personal computer approval
   systems life cycle implementation
   applications software selection
   applications software approval
   applications software standards
   end user support

Line Management Activities:

   applications prioritizing
   personal computer selection
   personal computer operation
   office systems operation
   external databases
   external timesharing

In this new corporate environment, the corporate IS group was given a charter to insure the competitive use of technology and to provide cost-effective utilities, while minimizing operational and technical risks and facilitating organizational flexibility. Included as "corporate utilities" are corporate computing facilities, generic applications (e.g., payroll), technical consulting/support services, and a contingency facility. Table 2.5 shows how IS activities were distributed across corporate and sector IS groups. This reorganization is very supportive of the trends noted in the CISR study.

TABLE 2.5   **MHC's Distribution of IT Management Responsibilities**

Activity	Corporate IS	Shared	Sector IS
STRATEGIC			
Strategic Planning & Control		X	
Marketplace Intelligence & Technology Research	X		
Architecture Planning			X
TACTICAL			
Resource Planning & Acquisition			X
Systems Development			X
Computer & Telecommunications Operations			X
Corporate Utilities	X		
INFRASTRUCTURE			
Policy & Standards Management	X		
Human Resource Management			X
Risk Management	X		

The Dilemma of IT Management

The results of the CISR survey and the MHC experience add support to the contention that a fourth era of IT management has begun. It is in adopting this view of the information economy within a business that today's major dilemma regarding IT management is raised: ". . . the need to simultaneously provide centralized direction and coordination while recognizing the value of increased discretion regarding IT decision making on the part of managers throughout the organization."[8] To exploit future IT opportunities, centralized direction and control of these diverse technologies is often required. On the other hand, many line managers have both the desire and ability to acquire, develop, and implement IT products and services without going through the corporate IS group; and they are doing so.

How, then, should an organization distribute its IT management responsibilities such that the benefits of both centralized coordination and line discretion are realized? It is clearly inappropriate either for the corporate IS group to strive to maintain a monopoly role or for each operating unit to fully control its own information destiny.[9] It is also apparent that any apportionment of IT management responsibilities must consider an organization's unique history and current situation.

Many issues must be examined in depth to gain insights into resolving this dilemma of IT management. How are organizations currently assigning their IT management responsibilities? To what extent does such an assignment depend on an organization's size, management orientation, or current use of IT? Will the assignment of responsibilities from divisional IS groups to line management follow that which is already occurring from the corporate IS to divisional IS groups? In what ways is the effective use of IT linked to these assignments of IT management responsibilities? As we are just now entering this fourth era of IT management, few guidelines are available for senior managers struggling with these issues. This research project produces such guidelines.

Notes

1. Examples can be found in many articles and books, including: Parsons, G.L., "Information Technology: A New Competitive Weapon," *Sloan Management Review,* Vol. 25, No. 1, 1983, 3-15; Porter, M.E. and Millar, V.E., "How Information Gives You Competitive Advantage," *Harvard Business Review,* Vol. 63, No. 4, 1985, 149-160.; Wiseman, Charles, *Strategy and Computers: Information Systems as Competitive Weapons,* Homewood, Ill.: Dow Jones-Irwin, 1985; Child, J., "Information Technology, Organization, and Response to Strategic Challenges," *California Management Review,* Vol. 30, No. 1, 1987, 33-50; and, Drucker, P. F., "The Coming of the New Organization," *Harvard Business Review,* Vol. 66, No. 1., 1988, 45-53.

2. The data for this table come from: Ein-Dor, P. and Segev, E., "Information Systems: Emergence of a New Organizational Function," *Information & Management,* Vol. 5, No. 4/5, 1982, 281.

3. This table is adapted from Table 2 of: Zmud, R.W., "Design Alternatives for Organizing Information Systems Activities," *MIS Quarterly,* Vol. 8, No. 2, 1984, 82.

4. For a more in-depth discussion of the concept of an information economy within a business, see: Zmud, R.W., Boynton, A.C., and Jacobs, G.C., "The Information Economy: A New Perspective for Effective Information Systems Management," *Data Base,* Vol. 16, No. 1, 1986, 17-23.

5. For examples of such "think" pieces, see: Buchanan, J.R. and Linowes, R.C., "Understanding Distributed Data Processing," *Harvard Business Review,* Vol. 58, No. 4, 1980, 143-153; Allen, B., "An Unmanaged Computer System Can Stop You Dead," *Harvard Business Review,* Vol. 60, No. 6, 1982, 76-87; and, Lucas, H.C., Jr., "Utilizing Information Technology: Guidelines for Managers," *Sloan Management Review,* Vol. 28, No. 1, 1986, 39-47.

6. Benjamin, R.I., Dickinson, C., Jr., and Rockart, J.F., "Changing Role of the Corporate Information Systems Officer," *MIS Quarterly,* Vol. 9, No. 3, 1985, 177-188.

7. La Belle, A. and Nyce, H.E., "Whither the IT Organization?" *Sloan Management Review*, Vol. 28, No. 4, 75-85.

8. Boynton, A.C. and Zmud, R.W., "Information Technology Planning in the 1990's: Directions for Research and Practice," *MIS Quarterly*, Vol. 11, No. 1, 1987, 61.

9. For a provocative essay predicting the demise of the corporate IS function, see: Dearden, J., "The Withering Away of the IS Organization," *Sloan Management Review*, Vol. 28, No. 4, 1987, 87-91.

3
Summarized Survey Findings

A total of 79 business units drawn from 35 companies responded to a comprehensive three-part survey. The majority of respondents were manufacturing firms, but the sample also included a few firms from the insurance, financial services, and telecommunications industries. Questions were posed to each business unit's senior executive, each company's CFO, and each company's senior IS executive (CIO). Detailed descriptions of the sampling strategy as well as the design of the survey questionnaire can be found in Appendix A. Appendices B, C, and D contain the questionnaires that were used.

Background Information on Survey Companies

To develop background information for an assessment of the patterns of IT decision making, respondents were asked for information about how the IS function was organized, the nature of their installed IT, their reliance on IT for both business operations and strategy, and the quality of the managerial relationships existing among corporate IS, divisional IS groups, and business units. The findings are presented in this chapter.

Organization of the IS Function

As mentioned in Chapter 2, most IS groups have been housed within the finance and accounting functions. This is still the case for many of the surveyed companies. However, a trend toward organizing the IS activity as a separate staff function reporting directly to senior management appeared. Most IS groups were managed as cost centers, but a few did operate as internal profit centers. Most charged a significant portion of their costs to users. At the divisional level, most IS groups (68 percent) reported to a business unit manager rather than to the corporate IS group.

Installed Information Technology

Our survey companies averaged almost 10 years of experience with data base systems and the use of outside data services (see Table 3.1.A). Additionally, most had installed microcomputers by the very early 1980s and have since introduced information centers, electronic mail and local area networks (LANs). However, a clear difference was observed between the installation of a technology and the pervasive use of this technology (see Table 3.1.B). While these companies were making extensive use of data base systems and interactive computing, only about 20 percent of their microcomputers were linked with local area networks and only 20 percent of applications were being developed using 4th generation languages. Our interpretation of these differences suggests that technologies are deployed relatively slowly. The survey data support a notion that six-to-eight years of experience with a technology may be required for the technology to achieve a 50 percent penetration level.

TABLE 3.1   **Technologies Installed in Sample Companies**

A.   Average year sample companies installed or established technologies

External Data Services	1979
Data Base Management System	1979
Data Base Administrator	1980
Microcomputers	1981
Information Center	1982
Electronic Mail	1982
Local Area Networker	1983

B.   Average penetration of technologies

	PERCENTAGE
Data Stored in DBMS	50
Interactive Applications	62
Microcomputers Attached to LANs	20
Applications Developed VIA 4th GLS	20

Reliance on Information Technology

Two observations can be made about the role of IT in supporting the activities of these companies (see Table 3.2). First, they are heavy users of IT in support of staff and operating activities. As expected, the application areas with the most extensive IT use involved finance and accounting. However, we also found significant reliance on IT in the support of customer service, logistics, and manufacturing. Second, few of these companies relied heavily on IT to support strategic activities. Enhancing customer linkages was the only strategic initiative

TABLE 3.2 **Business Unit Reliance on Information Technology**

	MEAN	EXTENT OF RELIANCE
FOR OPERATING ACTIVITIES:		
Customer Service	3.3	Moderate to Great
Logistics	3.2	Moderate to Great
Marketing	2.9	Moderate
Manufacturing	3.2	Moderate to Great
Sales	3.0	Moderate
FOR STAFF ACTIVITIES:		
Engineering	2.9	Moderate
Finance/Accounting	4.0	Great
Human Resources	2.7	Some to Moderate
Planning	3.0	Moderate
Treasury	2.9	Moderate
FOR STRATEGIC ACTIVITIES:		
Enhancing Customer Linkages	3.1	Moderate
Enhancing Existing Products	2.5	Some
Introducing New Products	2.4	Some
Being Low Cost Producer	2.9	Moderate
Having Manufacturing Flexibility	2.7	Some to Moderate
Entering New Markets	2.4	Some
Enhancing Supplier Linkages	2.4	Some
Providing Value Added Services	2.7	Some to Moderate

consistently addressed by these firms. Most of these companies do not appear as yet to view IT as a crucial component of their business strategies. The contrast between reliance on IT to support operating/staff activities and the reliance on IT to support strategy suggests that most companies are only now beginning to identify the potential linkages between IT and business strategy.

IS/Business Unit Relationships

We examined business unit relationships with corporate and divisional IS groups separately. While these relationships are good, significant differences do exist. In general, divisional IS groups are perceived as being more involved, having higher quality relationships, understanding the business units better, and agreeing more closely with business units on IT needs than are corporate IS groups. Such findings are consistent with the overall theme of this report—that decentralization of certain IS activities can result in more effective applications of IT products and services.

Location of IT Decision Responsibility

Patterns in IT management responsibilities were examined in two ways:

— By type of management group (non-IS corporate, IS corporate, non-IS business unit, and IS business unit)

— By type of IT decision (hardware, applications software, project management, and day-to-day operations)

As will be shown, the survey companies exhibited quite similar overall patterns across both management groups and decisions.

Analysis by Management Group

Corporate IS played a strong role in both long- and short-run hardware decisions; but business unit IS groups played a stronger role in decisions about new applications, IT project management, and day-to-day IS operations. Business unit managers (non-IS) had a strong role only in determining short-run applications.

A great deal of shared decision making was observed across all the decision types. Of particular interest was the extent to which business unit IS managers shared in decisions, both vertically with the corporate IS group and horizontally with non-IS managers in their business unit. Our interpretation is that business unit IS managers currently occupy a very traditional staff role and, thus, have not assumed a more central IT decision-making role. Key strategic decisions are made by the corporate IS groups; and key application decisions are made by non-IS business unit managers. Business unit IS groups implement (project management decisions) and operate (day-to-day IS operations decisions). Such observations were documented in the case studies.

Trends observed in the case studies suggest this role for business unit IS groups may become pervasive. Corporate IS groups appear to be increasingly committed to direction setting for new technology and certain long-run application decisions. Non-IS business unit management appears to be assuming a stronger role in application decisions and IT project management. The trends appear to leave two options for business unit IS groups. Either business unit IS managers will become important members of their unit's management team through their technological skills and leadership, or business unit IS groups increasingly will become purveyors of commodity IT services.

Analysis by Decision Type

Most decisions about mainframes and minicomputers were centered in the corporate IS group. However, corporate IS was more involved in long-run hardware decisions than short-run hardware decisions. The exception to this pattern involved microcomputer decisions, which most often were handled in the business units with the business unit IS group serving a dominant role.

In contrast, application decisions were shared between non- IS business unit management and the business unit IS group. The only exceptions to such a pattern involved application areas, such as finance, treasury or accounting, which typically require corporate-wide solutions. Responsibility for applications requiring corporate-wide solutions tended to be located in the corporate IS groups (an observation supported in the case studies).

Project management decisions tended to reside in business unit IS groups, but they were often shared with either corporate IS or non-IS business unit managers. Interestingly, the case studies indicated that implementation was likely to be most successful when non-IS business unit managers were given project management responsibility.

Operating decisions were centered in the business unit IS groups. However, both corporate IS groups and business unit managers shared in these decisions. It is interesting to note that here, as with other issues, the CIO respondents rated their involvement in operating decisions much higher than did the business unit managers.

Summary

These results (summarized in Table 3.3) provide consistent evidence that the location of decision making differs depending on the type of decision to be made and who is affected by the decision. Decisions that affect corporate-wide service delivery (such as acquiring new technology, adding to capacity, or building a common application) can be, are, and perhaps should be the responsibility of the corporate IS group. Decisions that are specific to a business unit (such as marketing applications) can be, are, and perhaps should be the responsibility of that business unit. The implication is that assignment of IT decision responsibility is both complex and conditional. It must reflect a balance between the needs of the whole organization for commonality, economy, and clear IT direction-setting, while, at the same time, retaining the flexibility required to be responsive to local business unit needs.

TABLE 3.3 **Who Makes IS Decisions**

DECISIONS	*WHO MAKES DECISION*
Hardware	Corporate IS
Long-run Application	Shared Between Business Unit IS and Business Unit Management
Short-run Application	Business Unit Managers
Project Management	Business Unit IS Manager
Operations of IS	Business Unit IS Manager

These findings suggest that technology direction setting is a corporate responsibility, but that decisions targeted at "day-to-day business activities" should be made as close to the user as possible. The results also support the notion that effective IT decision making should be a highly interactive process with corporate and divisional IS groups as well as business unit managers actively sharing in the decision-making process.

IT Decision Making and Reliance on IT

While similar overall patterns in IT decision making were observed, the survey companies did differ in the extent to which IT decision making had been decentralized. (Detailed discussion of these differences can be found in Chapter 7.) We analyzed these differences to discover if the apportionment of IT decision making seemed to have an impact on business unit reliance on IT to carry out operating activities or to support strategy.

Several broad observations result. Generally, more reliance on IT in supporting both line operations and strategic initiatives was observed in those companies that delegated a large portion of IT decision making to business units. This was particularly true when short-run IT decisions were made at the business unit level. However, we were unable to draw similar conclusions about the location of IT decision making and the use of IT in supporting staff activities because of the variability in staff function reporting relationships.

The above remarks address the question of locating IT decision making at the corporate or business unit level. It is more difficult to arrive at a clear recommendation regarding the assignment of IT decision-making responsibilities within the business unit itself, that is, to IS or non-IS managers within the business unit. Although we found greater reliance on IT when non-IS managers were involved with IT application decisions, we also observed high reliance on IT when the business unit IS group shared in application decisions and when the business unit IS group retained primary responsibility for project management and operations. This implies that penetration of IT into the business unit is best fostered when the business unit IS group manages the technology but *actively involves* or *relies on* non-IS business unit managers in making application decisions.

IT Decision Making and IS/User Relations

Information services/user relationships are important because of a common belief (borne out in the case studies) that the IS/user relationships will affect the quality and acceptability of new applications. Better relationships, higher levels of non-IS manager involvement in IS decisions, and shared assessments of IT needs and opportunities are all believed to contribute to the more effective use of IT. As a result, we were interested in the influence of decentralizing IT decisions on IS/user relationships.

The results indicated that higher quality relations are more likely to develop between a business unit's IS group and its non-IS managers than between the corporate IS and these non-IS managers. Such an observation was largely independent of the location of IT decision-making responsibility. Business unit managers believed business unit IS groups provided service of higher quality, greater reliability and on a more timely basis than was provided by corporate IS. Further, they believed business unit IS groups agreed more with them on IT goals, needs, and priorities.

There are two findings that did depend on the location of IT decision responsibility. First, the business units believed corporate IS agreed with them regarding the business unit's needs and opportunities more when IT decision making was centralized. Second, business unit non-IS managers were more likely to be involved with IS activities when IT decision making was decentralized.

Overall, these results suggest that business unit IS groups are more likely than corporate IS to develop and maintain the high quality relations with users that are required to promote effective IT use. As a consequence, the movement of application, project, and operating decisions to business unit IS groups is likely to foster better use of IT.

4
Summarized Case
Study Findings

Examinations of the IT decision-making strategies of eight firms were conducted with two main objectives in mind:

1. To enable a deeper analysis than is possible through survey techniques.

2. To better understand the forces that underlie these strategies.

Accordingly, interviews were held with the senior IS executive and the divisional IS directors in each case study firm. See Chapter 9 for detailed descriptions of each case site and Appendix A for details on the research procedures.

This chapter begins with short descriptions of the major observations about each case study firm. Key findings across all eight case sites are then interpreted to identify consistent themes appearing in these firms' IT decision-making strategies.

General Observations

The primary criterion used to select the case study sites was a firm's IT decision-making pattern as revealed through the survey results (see Chapter 3 for a summary of these findings and Chapter 7 for a detailed discussion). Of the eight firms that were selected as case study sites, the following distributions were noted:

— Two exhibited an *average* pattern of IT decision making based on our analysis of survey data; that is, the involvement of corporate IS, business unit IS, and line management was similar to "average" responses obtained in the field survey.

— Two exhibited a *shared* pattern of IT decision making; that is, corporate IS, divisional IS, and line management shared involvement in many, if not most, IT management responsibilities.

— Two exhibited a *centralized* pattern of IT decision making. That is, corporate IS was primarily responsible for IT management.

— Two exhibited a *decentralized* pattern of IT decision making; that is, managers in the business units were primarily responsible for IT management.

Table 4.1 identifies these firms according to our selection scheme but also indicates that this "initial" categorization was not very precise. IT decision-making strategies tend to be both complex and bound to idiosyncrasies within each company. While common overall patterns do exist, each company's own strategy is fairly unique.

TABLE 4.1   **IT Decison-making Strategies of the Case Study Firms**

Firm	From Survey Responses	From Case Study Analysis
A	average	shared
B	shared	decentralized
C	shared	divisionalized
D	decentralized	average
E	decentralized	divisionalized
F	centralized	shared
G	centralized	centralized
H	average	shared

It was also deemed desirable that the case study firms differ from one another along other attributes, such as size, organizational structure, IT sophistication, and IT use. As shown in Tables 4.2 and 4.3, the case study firms do, in fact, differ along these lines. The eight firms, four of which are large (A, B, C, and D) and four of which are small (E, F, G, and H), represent eight different manufacturing industries. Also, a special effort was taken to ensure that no selected firm was in financial difficulty.

Corporation A

It is difficult to characterize Corporation A (CORP-A) as centralized or decentralized in its IT decision making. While the corporate IS group plays a heavy role in setting corporate-wide policies and standards, in practice these policies and standards are formed by a consensus of operating group IS directors where operating groups are comprised of several business units in the same industry.

TABLE 4.2   **General Characteristics of Case Study Firms**

Firms	Revenue ($millions)	Geographic Locations	Growth Vehicle	Corporate Management Style
A	3,250	many	internal	decentralized
B	2,500	many	internal	decentralized
C	1,500	few	internal + acquisition	toward decentralized
D	1,000	many	internal	toward decentralized
E	600	many	internal + acquisition	centralized
F	420	few	internal	toward decentralized
G	230	few	internal	centralized
H	200	many	internal	decentralized

TABLE 4.3   **Technology Characteristics of Case Study Firms**

Firms	Technology Adopter	Technical Sophistication	IT Use for Operations	IT Use for Strategy
A	very early	average	good	good
B	very early	exceptional	good	fair
C	early	good	good	fair
D	early	exceptional	mixed	good
E	average	below average	very good	fair
F	mixed	exceptional	very good	fair
G	late	exceptional	very good	good
H	average	exceptional	very good	good

In a similar vein, operating group IS directors report to the operating group executives rather than corporate IS. However, business unit IS directors report to the operating group IS directors. The firm's rationale for this mixed model, which is consistent across layers of the company, is that it promotes synergy in technology and applications while maintaining the benefits of autonomy where unique applications are appropriate.

A strong opinion was expressed that steering committees are a very useful way to coordinate IS, obtain line manager involvement in IT decision making, and obtain shared (IS staff and line management) decisions and commitments. In fact, steering committees are viewed as the integrative mechanism in such a large, decentralized environment. Cost pressures add increased importance to the role of these committees in coordinating planning and seeking out common technologies and applications. To be successful, these committees must be composed of individuals who know both the technology and the business. The downside of this approach is that it becomes possible to ". . . share life away and get nothing done."

The autonomy at the operating group level creates great diversity in the involvement of line managers in IT decision making; however, some business unit IS managers have chosen to involve line managers more than others. Corporate IS is concerned that too much decentralization may result in inefficiency, redundancy, lack of commitment to common applications, and a reduced capability to introduce major IT changes throughout the corporation. However, corporate IS management fully expects CORP-A to continue on a moderate path toward further decentralization.

Corporation B

A transition to decentralization has occurred over the past ten years at Corporation B (CORP-B). Currently, most IS activities are directed by line managers and handled by divisional IS staff. The corporate IS group primarily serves an advisory role. The major driving force behind this decentralization is an overall organizational philosophy favoring decentralization as a managerial strategy for coping with the specialty markets in which the firm now competes. The major benefit from decentralization is that the divisions are able to tailor divisional information systems to fit divisional needs.

Interviewees expressed considerable agreement with this strategy. Some mentioned a desire, however, to receive more direction from the corporate IS group regarding IT use. This might be reflected in the observation that CORP-B has not been as successful in supporting business strategic initiatives as it has been in supporting business operations.

The prior era of centralized information technology management was seen by interviewees as a major factor that enabled CORP-B to build the strong technological base now being exploited through decentralization. Another interesting observation was that line managers tend to become more proactive in directing and controlling IT use as they gain confidence in the technology and in their ability to apply the technology. This seems to occur from exposure and experience with IT and from having the divisional IS director report to the division's general manager rather than its controller.

Corporation C

Corporation C (CORP-C) has moved toward decentralization in the past few years, but this move primarily has involved a shift in IT decision-making responsibilities from the corporate IS group to divisional IS groups. Currently, most IS activities are handled by the divisional IS groups. The primary role of the corporate IS group is to support these divisional IS groups. Line management, generally, is not very involved in IT decision making. The major forces behind this move to decentralize IT decision making are an overall organizational philosophy favoring decentralization and improvements in the technology itself that economically enable decentralization. The divisions that experienced more extensive decentralization of IT decision making were described as those having the most experience with decentralization and those in which the divisional IS director reports to the division's general manager rather than its controller.

The major benefit obtained from decentralization is that applications implemented within the divisions better fit divisional information needs. However, those interviewed expressed a general belief that CORP-C was not applying IT in an aggressive manner. This was attributed partially to the limited line management involvement and to a recognition that more progress was needed in developing "partnership" relations between the IS staff and line management.

Corporation D

A strong move to decentralization of IS has occurred at Corporation D (CORP-D) in the past six years. Corporate IS now plays a minor role in business unit IT decisions. A new management team and a changing business climate were the major forces behind this new acceptance of overall decentralization. The principle benefit from decentralization has been the ability to meet user information needs with better, faster IT solutions. Corporate IS is very comfortable with its limited role, and business unit IS is comfortable not only with its high level of IT decision responsibility but also with its accountability for achieving results.

The degree of decentralization differs somewhat across business units. The more diversified and geographically dispersed the business units are, the more they are decentralized. Those with more homogeneous products or operations are more likely to have greater business unit level, rather than line manager, involvement in IT decision making. Smaller business units are likely to be more centralized with respect to hardware and, in some cases, IS personnel. This reflects the need for a critical mass to justify placement of personnel.

Corporation E

Most IS activities at Corporation E (CORP-E) are handled by divisional IS staffs. Line managers, with much IS guidance, are responsible for proposing projects. As a result, there is virtually no corporate IS role and only minimal line manager IS responsibility. The forces behind such a division of IT decision-making responsibility are the firm's acquisition growth strategy, a corporate philosophy that supports lean management staffs, and the perceived costs of centralization.

It is unlikely that any changes will occur in the immediate future. Fairly strong convictions exist that IS activities are a staff, rather than line, responsibility and are best handled locally.

The major benefit perceived from this division of responsibility is the ability of each division to tailor applications precisely to its information needs. The inefficiency of such a strategy, however, was recognized as was the potential of such a strategy to inhibit innovative uses of IT.

Corporation F

Corporation F (CORP-F) makes use of a more highly interactive computing environment than most of the survey companies. Approximately one-half of all managerial employees have terminals, tied directly into the firm's central computer system, at their desks. Much of the software in use has been developed by line personnel using a fourth-generation language but spending no more than 20 percent of their time on IS activities. This prevalence of user-developed applications, along with a corporate policy of not charging business units for their use of the central computer system, has resulted in a high degree of decentralization.

The senior IS executive at CORP-F is a member of a senior management team of about 30 individuals who work in the same location and operate with a high degree of interaction (formal and informal). Corporate IS has chosen to establish the hardware environment and to oversee application projects only when outside vendors are involved or when the corporate IS group is invited to actively participate in a development effort. Having established the hardware environment, the lean corporate IS group is content primarily to consult and advise, stepping in as a developer only when appropriate and asked. CORP-F believes this strategy has worked well for them given their size and the homogeneity of their business. They believe the extensive involvement of users in application development has played a key role in their high level of IT use. At the same time, they do not believe their small size permits cost-effective decentralization of hardware decisions or that their homogeneous business units require differentiated hardware.

Corporation G

Most of Corporation G's (CORP-G) IS activities, aside from application development, are handled by the corporate IS staff. However, application development occurs within very tight operational and developmental architectures specified by the corporate IS group. Although there is a desire that line managers should become more involved with these activities, the divisional IS staffs handle most development and implementation activities. The primary role of line management lies in project initiation and approval. The main reason for the relatively recent decentralization of application development was to improve what were peceived as quite poor IS/user relations.

While the advantages of dispersing certain IT decisions are recognized, further decentralization is unlikely to occur soon. Concern was expressed, for example, that decentralization is more expensive in terms of IS staffing; and it is not clear that CORP-G can afford the additional expense.

Corporation H

A transition toward more decentralized IT decision making is occurring at Corporation H (CORP-H). Business units are increasingly responsible for proposing, prioritizing, and managing the development of applications. Corporate IS staff will continue to handle most IS activities other than application development. The driving force behind the decentralization of applications decisions has been the need to align IT applications with business strategies. Aligning IT applications is perceived to require greater involvement by business unit managers in application decisions as well as greater knowledge of business units by IS staff analysts.

Cost is a limiting factor in the degree of decentralization that can be realized. None of the CORP-H business units is large enough to support full-time, comprehensive IS groups. Economies of scale are realized by retaining activities at the corporate level that are common to all business units. It is in the area of application initiation and development that they believe the greatest benefits from decentralization can accrue. Thus, their first moves in that direction involved pushing both applications decisions and systems analysts into the business units.

An additional factor that influences the manner by which IT management responsibilities are apportioned at CORP-H is the physical isolation of many of the firm's operations. A number of its plants are located in remote places. The size of these installations does not justify large local IS staffs to support the installed technology. At the same time, placement of only one or two IS staff members in remote locations leads to personal and professional isolation.

Major Themes

Three overall themes are evident in these case studies. First, seven of these eight firms are moving many, if not most, IT management responsibilities from the corporate IS group to both divisional IS groups and line managers. Significant changes that have occurred in the past few years are expected to continue occurring, particularly with IT planning and application development.

As might be expected, we observed differences in patterns of IT management responsibility between the large and small firms. Table 4.4 provides a summary profile of these patterns. Given the criteria by which firms were selected, the large firms are surprisingly consistent. This was not the case with the small firms, most likely because of resource constraints and a limited flexibility in acquiring and applying IT resources. Even so, line managers of both large and small firms are becoming much more actively involved in targeting IT use.

TABLE 4.4   **Overall Pattern of IT Decision Making**

	FIRM SIZE	
CORPORATE LEVEL	Large	Small
Corporate IS	* IT strategic planning * corporate IT standards * corporate systems * IT oversight * advisory * IT utilities	* IT planning * development * operations
Divisional IS	* IT planning * development * operations * project management	* development * project management
Line Management	* set priorities * initiate projects * project management * specify needs	* set priorities * initiate projects * project management * specify needs

A second theme is that the business units most effective in their IT use tended to be those whose IS staffs or line managers were more involved in IT decision making. This was most pronounced where line management had assumed major roles in the business unit's IS activities. Interestingly, line management involvement is linked with increased experience and success in IS activities. It also intensifies when the divisional IS staff reports to a division's senior line executive rather than either the corporate IS group or the division's controller.

A third overall theme is that a firm's success in developing strategic systems seems to be inhibited by decentralization. Pushing IT decision making into the business units does enable line managers to target applications to current opportunities and problems. What seems to suffer, however, are concerted efforts to maintain or extend the technology base on which strategic systems depend and the ability to adopt long-term or fresh perspectives in IT planning.

Apparently, success with strategic systems requires corporate (or divisional) strategic IT planning efforts to be established and then linked with knowledgable and involved line managers.

The importance of these three themes is emphasized by the critical success factors (CSFs) mentioned by interviewees in the eight firms. Interviewees were asked to identify those factors critical to both IT success and IT failure in their organization. Table 4.5 lists these CSFs by the frequency each was mentioned. Notice the first two CSFs: the capabilities of the IS staff and the capabilities of line management. IT success requires both talented IS personnel, who understand the "business of the business," and talented line managers, who recognize the potential value of IT and are actively involved in applying this technology to their operational and managerial work systems. Each of the next two CSFs is associated with building an environment supportive of the development of talented IS staff and talented line managers. In large firms, this supportive environment is an outgrowth of senior management support. In smaller firms, it is an outgrowth of financial support. The fifth CSF, synergistic IS staff and line manager relations, likely derives from the first four and the last: a firm's IT management strategy.

TABLE 4.5 **Critical Success Factors**

	FIRMS							
	A	*B*	*C*	*D*	*E*	*F*	*G*	*H*
FACTORS								
Capabilities of the IS staff	X	X	X	X	X	X	X	X
Capabilities of line managers		X	X	X	X		X	X
Organizational environment	X	X	X	X				
Financial environment					X	X	X	
IS staff/line manager relations			X	X				X
IT management strategy	X			X				

The final set of issues explored in these case studies involved the identification of the major forces influencing the IT management strategies of the firms. Six consistent rationales were revealed in the interviews. These are listed in Table 4.6, again in order of the frequency each was mentioned. The first rationale explains why IT responsibilities are moved into business units: to get both IS staff and IT decision making "closer" to a business's operations and strategies. Moving the IS staff into operating units permits these employees to develop a better understanding of business activities and tighter relations with line managers. Dispersing IT decision making to line managers provides both motivation and personal accountability for IT investments. Further, it is unrealistic to ask line managers to "bet their careers" on new IT applications and then place control of

TABLE 4.6   **Rationale Underling Patterns of IT Management**

FACTORS	A	B	C	D	E	F	G	H
Move IS "closer to business"	X	X	X	X	X	X		X
Corporate management style	X	X	X	X	X		X	
Heterogeneous information needs	X	X	X	X		X	X	
Economies of scale	X			X	X	X		X
Technological advances			X	X		X		X
Corporate acquisition history			X	X	X			

(column group header: FIRMS)

this technology in a staff (e.g., a corporate or divisional IS group) unit.

The second rationale reflects our observation that the extent of IT management decentralization tends to follow the overall corporate style of decision making. The third rationale shows that decisions about IT use are closely tied to the organization's information processing needs. If all business units have similar needs, centralization is often an appropriate strategy. However, decentralization seems more appropriate where business unit activities, and hence the information needs of each, diverge.

The fourth rationale, economies of scale, primarily applies to the advantages of centralization in smaller firms. Often, it simply is not economically feasible for small firms to disperse scarce, expensive IT resources, such as personnel, throughout the organization. The fifth rationale recognizes that it would have been impossible to decentralize many IT managerial responsibilities without the technical advancements that have produced today's relatively inexpensive but highly reliable and easy-to-use IT products and services.

The last rationale acknowledges the significant role that a firm's growth strategy can play in determining its IT management strategy. When a firm acquires a business unit, the acquired unit's IS staff is often left intact rather than absorbed into the firm's current IT management strategy.

This last rationale also introduces our final observation. In order to begin to understand why a firm has adopted a particular managerial strategy, it is necessary to uncover at least a portion of its corporate history. Growth strategies, new senior management teams, economic downturns, changes in corporate direction, strong managerial personalities, and the actions of competitors, suppliers and customers all affect a firm's managerial strategies.

As would be expected, corporate history was extremely influential in establishing the IT management strategies of these eight firms. Given this, the consistency observed in IT decision-making trends throughout the case study sites is both fascinating and significant. American industry does in fact seem to be entering a fourth era of IT management—that of the "information economy" described in Chapter 2.

5
Management Guidelines

In describing the findings from the analysis of survey data and from the case studies, we observed several consistent trends in IT decision making. Most notable of these is a distinct trend toward greater involvement of non-IS managers in IT decisions. This is particularly true when new IT applications are applied to operating level activities and to external interfaces with customers and suppliers. There appears to be a strong consensus that pushing application decisions out of the IS group toward users is the only viable strategy in the current environment. A second strong trend is that of moving short-run IT decisions concerning hardware, IT project management, and IT operations from the corporate IS group to business unit IS groups. However, corporate IS management recognizes its need to retain long-run IT decisions, as well as decisions about applications that are common across business units, to control both the technology and associated costs.

These trends are moderated by company history, size, and philosophy concerning decentralization. Historical events such as mergers and acquisitions play a strong role in determining the management of IT. For example, acquired business units are much more likely to retain responsibility for their own IT decision making. Company policies on decentralization of decision making also have an effect on how IT decision responsibilities are apportioned. Finally, size may limit the opportunities for decentralization. Similarly, there are economies of scale in certain IS activities, such as the operation of a computational utility or large-scale programming projects, which may limit the opportunities for decentralizing certain IS activities in small companies.

Six key guidelines regarding IT decision making can be drawn from this study:

1. *Decentralization of short-run IT decisions tends to be associated with higher performing business units.* Firms that exhibit more decentralization in their short run IT decision making tend to rely on IT to a greater extent in

supporting operating activities and tend to have higher quality relations between their IS groups and their non-IS managers.

2.   *The strategic use of IT requires the active involvement of corporate IS, divisional IS, and line managers in IT decision making.* The case study results provide ample evidence that decentralization may inhibit efforts to extend IT to support new strategic thrusts. On the other hand, the survey results indicate a greater use of IT in support of strategy when IT decisions are delegated to business units. These two results can be reconciled by carefully differentiating the roles played by managers across all three levels. The case study results identify the corporate IS role as one of introducing new technology or identifying the opportunities for IT to play a role in accomplishing strategy. The survey results then suggest that line management's role is one of shaping the business opportunity to apply the technology; and the business unit IS role is one of providing required technical skills to implement the technology.

3.   *Higher involvement of line managers in IT decision making tends to be associated with greater business unit performance, a greater reliance by the business unit on IT, and better quality IS/user relations.*

4.   *Greater line manager involvement in IT decision making occurs when the divisional IS manager reports to the division's senior executive rather than the division's controller.* Apparently, locating a divisional IS group under the division's controller communicates a message to line managers that IS activities are a staff, rather than a line, responsibility.

5.   *The retention of decision responsibility by divisional IS groups for IT project management and IT operations tends to be associated with higher business unit performance and a greater reliance by business units on the use of IT to support both operations and strategies.* The case studies indicated that some companies are beginning to assign responsibility for IT project management to non-IS managers in the belief that better results will result. Organizations may wish to think carefully about the implications of such a responsibility assignment.

6.   *Higher quality relations invariably develop between users and divisional IS staff than between users and corporate IS staff.*

In conclusion, this study provides evidence to strongly support the view expressed in Chapter 2 that certain IT management responsibilities should be moved both lower in the organization and out to line managers. Even more justification for dispersing IT decision-making responsibility to line managers will appear as these individuals become increasingly skilled in applying information technologies and as technology advances. The real challenge for corporate management is to strike a balance between the increasing opportunities for and benefits of decentralization with the need to plan for and coordinate the introduction of new technology over the long run. The corporate IS group will continue to play a critical role, but it is likely to be a role of policy setting and staff consulting on new technology and corporate-wide applications. Over time, we expect divisional IS groups to serve less important roles in IT planning and application development but to continue serving an essential organizational role in managing and operating installed technology.

Part II
Detailed Analysis of the Survey Responses and the Case Study Interviews

6
Survey Findings: Company Characteristics

This chapter describes the surveyed companies. Such information serves two roles. First, it provides a context with which to interpret many of the study's findings. Of second, and more general, interest is the "snapshot" it provides of how a broad spectrum of companies are currently applying IT, and of how these companies have organized their IS activities.

Overall Company Characteristics

As mentioned in an earlier chapter, completed questionnaires were received from 79 business units drawn from 35 companies. Most were manufacturing companies representing industries from consumer products to heavy manufacturing. Service firms responding included representatives from the insurance, financial services, and telecommunications industries. Firms ranged in size from $54 million to $12 billion in sales.

The survey firms, on average, were growing faster than the economy as a whole (See Figure 6.1). However, average growth rates were declining from about 15 percent in 1984 to 5 percent in 1986. As shown in Figure 6.2, average return on assets for the sample was approximately 8 percent.

Company performance was assessed two other ways. First, each firm was asked to rate its current performance as a percentage of its ideal performance. Most respondents indicated their firms were performing at 70 to 80 percent of ideal. Second, each firm was asked what percentage of firms in that industry it outperformed. On average, the survey firms believed they were outperforming their competitors. The worst performing firms indicated they were outperforming the bottom 30 percent of their industry, and several indicated they were outperforming 90 percent or more of their competitors.

FIGURE 6.1   **Average Sales Growth Rates**

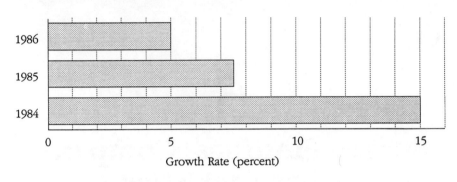

Growth Rate (percent)

FIGURE 6.2   **Average Return on Assets**

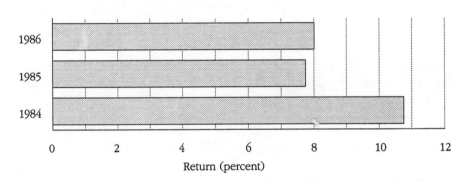

Return (percent)

Companies also were asked to depict their corporate management decision-making culture through a set of questions designed to elicit the degree to which decision authority across a range of functional areas was held by corporate management or business unit management. Figure 6.3 shows mean responses for each of nine functional areas. Here, a high positive value indicates that functional decisions are made at the corporate level (i.e., centralized), a large negative value indicates that functional decisions are made at the business unit (i.e., decentralized). A value of approximately zero indicates a shared decision. Of interest is the high degree of centralization for the treasury and finance/accounting functions and the high degree of decentralization for the customer service, marketing, and sales functions.

Organization of the IS Function

Traditionally, the information systems group has been housed within the finance/accounting function. This still appears to be the case in many firms, with

FIGURE 6.3   **Firm Centralization or Decentralization**

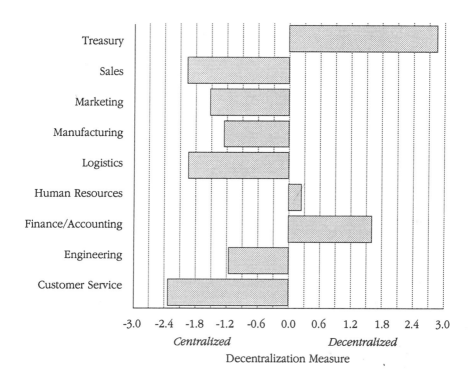

most of the senior IS executives (CIOs) in the survey companies reporting to either their firms' controllers or chief financial officers. However, several were in a separate staff function and reported to a vice-president for administration. Approximately one in five of the CIOs was a member of his company's executive committee.

The corporate IS function was structured in a number of ways. Six percent of our sample was organized as profit centers with bottom line responsibility. However, the vast majority (90 percent) was organized as cost centers. Of these, about two-thirds allocated IS costs to users.

Divisional IS groups reported through a variety of structures. The most common structure was for the divisional IS director to report to a business unit manager (controller, general manager, etc.). Sixty-eight percent of the companies were organized in this fashion. Of these, a little more than one half had a "dotted line" reporting relationship to the corporate IS group. In about 68 percent of the sample (mostly the smaller firms), divisional IS directors reported to corporate IS.

Figure 6.4 presents the size distribution of the IS staffs of the survey

FIGURE 6.4   **Number of Sample Firms with Indicated Total IS Staff Headcount**

| | Number of Firms Reporting | |
Headcount	Corporate IS Headcount	Firmwide IS Headcount
Less than 25	6	2
25–49	8	5
50–74	3	3
75–99	4	0
100–199	5	5
200–499	3	9
500–999	0	1
over 1000	4	7

companies. Most firms had fewer than 100 people in the corporate IS group with about 40 percent having fewer than 50 people. The typical company had a total head count of between 100 and 500. However, several companies had very large headcounts (over 1000) while one company had only seven. At least two reasons might explain this wide range in the size of these companies' IS staff. First, they obviously reflect differences in the absolute size of the companies: As would be expected, larger companies had larger IS staffs. Second, and more interesting, the differences also were based on differences in how IT is used and how applications are developed. Heavy reliance on fourth generation languages, which enable users to develop their own applications, and a limited IT role are two precursors of smaller IS staffs.

Installed Technology

The survey companies are applying current technology. Figure 6.5 presents the average year in which specific technologies were installed by the survey companies, and Figure 6.6 captures the extent current technologies are in widespread use within these firms. The data lead to observation that technologies are deployed rather slowly in organizations. While DBMS technology had been introduced in most firms by 1979, on average only about 50 percent of these firms' production data were being maintained in a DBMS in 1986. Similarly, only about 20 percent of the micros in these firms were linked through LANs by 1986 although most had introduced LAN technology by 1983. While these data do not warrant a strong conclusion about the rate at which appropriate technologies move from introduction to absorption, a period of at least six to eight years seems to be indicated.

FIGURE 6.5   **Average Year Technology Adopted**

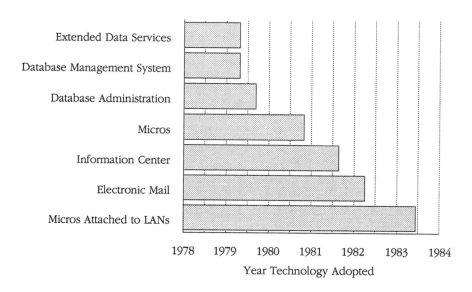

FIGURE 6.6   **Penetration of Technologies**

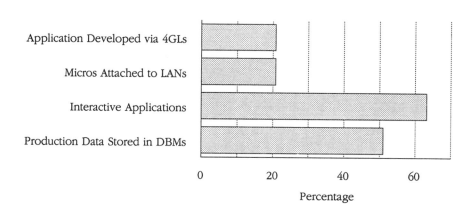

Reliance on Technology

Each business unit manager was asked to indicate the extent that line and staff activities relied on IT support. The activities selected included inbound/outbound logistics, manufacturing, marketing, sales, customer service, personnel/human resources, engineering/R&D, planning, finance/accounting, and treasury. Responses are shown in Figures 6.7 through 6.10. Figures 6.7 and 6.9 provide mean responses while Figures 6.8 and 6.10 provide distributions for these

FIGURE 6.7   **Business Unit Reliance on IT for Operating Activities**

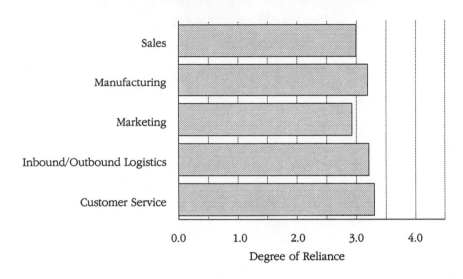

responses. In these figures, a "1" indicates no reliance on IT for an activity while a "5" indicates very great reliance.

It is clear that the survey companies rely on IT most heavily for finance/accounting activities. The firms also tended to rely on IT for customer service, inbound/outbound logistics, and manufacturing; however, this use is perhaps best characterized as being "moderate" and shows considerable variation across business units. Marketing, sales, engineering, planning, and treasury rely somewhat less on IT, with personnel relying the least. Noteworthy are the distributions for treasury and logistics. Both have bimodal distributions indicating that business unit dependence on IT for treasury and logistics activities was either heavy or light but not moderate.

Business unit managers also were asked to indicate the extent to which they relied on IT for accomplishing eight types of "strategic thrusts": enhancing customer linkages, enhancing existing products, introducing new products, becoming a low-cost producer, providing manufacturing flexibility, entering new markets, enhancing supplier linkages, and providing value-added services. Again, the range of possible responses was from no reliance to very great reliance (see Figures 6.11 and 6.12). The only strategic thrust for which IT played more than a moderate role, on average, is that of enhancing customer linkages. IT appeared to be moderately important for supporting a strategy of becoming a low-cost producer but was less important for the other strategic thrusts. For the whole sample, only about 5 percent of responses indicated very great reliance on IT for accomplishing any of the eight strategic thrusts; another 17 percent

FIGURE 6.8   **Reliance on IT for Operating Activities**

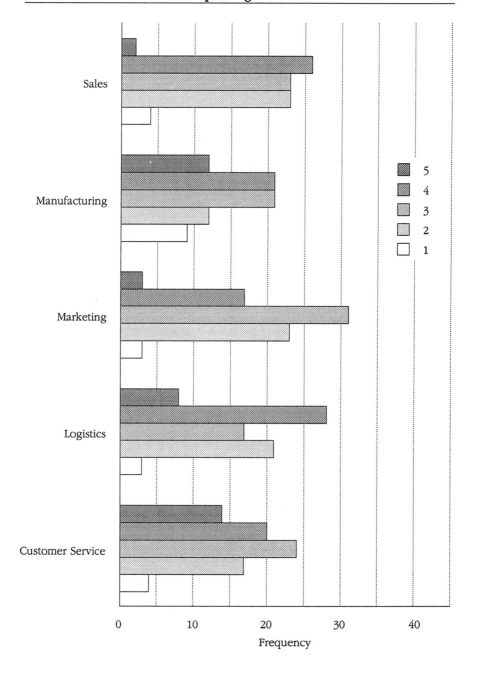

FIGURE 6.9   **Business Unit Reliance on IT for Staff Activities**

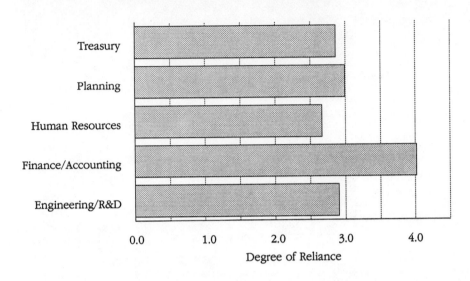

indicated great reliance on IT. Very few of the business units surveyed appear to be using IT as a fundamental part of implementing business strategy.

Quality of IS/User Relations

The CIO of each survey company as well as the senior executives of three business units in the company responded to a series of questions describing aspects of the quality of the relations that existed between IS staff and users.

A major interest involved the perceptions regarding the following:

—The extent to which the services delivered by corporate IS are of high quality;

—The extent to which corporate IS carried out its commitments;

—The extent to which corporate IS is involved in planning or acquiring IT products and services for business units;

—The extent of agreement between corporate IS and the business units on their IT needs and directions; and

—The extent to which corporate IS understood the business units' activities.

There were five possible responses to each question, which ranged from none to very great.

Table 6.1 presents the mean responses by each company's CIO and business

FIGURE 6.10 **Reliance on IT for Staff Activities**

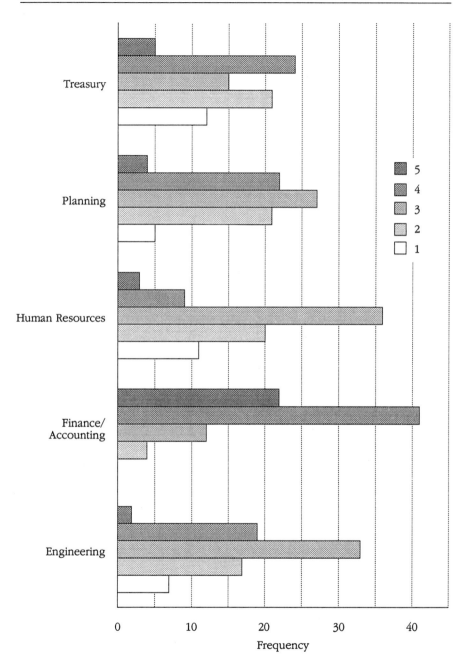

FIGURE 6.11 **Business Unit Reliance on IT for Strategic Activities**

Degree of Reliance

TABLE 6.1 **Comparison of CIOs' and Business Unit Managers' Perceptions of Corporate IS Group**

	CIO View	Business Unit View	Difference
1. Reliability Quality Timeliness	3.74	3.37	.36
2. Extent Commitments Carried Out	3.49	3.23	.26
3. Involvement in Planning, Acquiring, Proposing IT Services	2.96	2.71	.25
4. Agreement on Needs, Opportunities, Goals, Priorities	3.27	2.86	.41
5. IS Group's Understanding of Operations, Strategies, Management Practices	2.99	2.53	.46

Scale: 1 = None
3 = Moderate
5 = Very Great

FIGURE 6.12 **Reliance on IT for Strategic Activities**

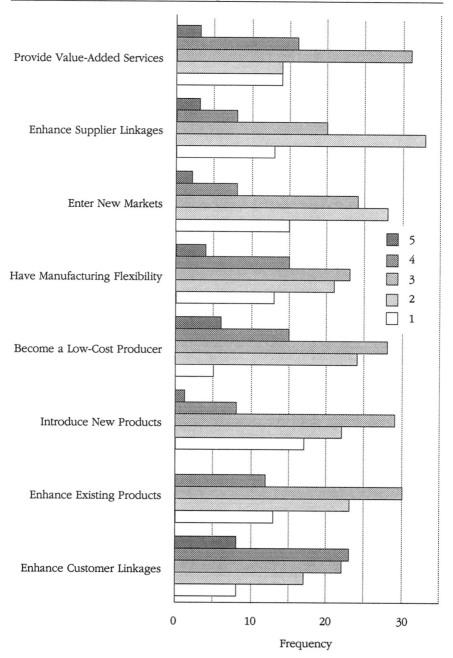

unit managers. Both perspectives viewed the IT services provided by the corporate IS group as being reliable, of good quality, and on time. Similarly, both tended to regard the corporate IS group as keeping its commitments. However, on average, corporate IS was only moderately involved in planning IT and acquiring IT resources at the business unit level. This moderate involvement may explain the gap between the CIO's view and the business unit managers' views of how well corporate IS agrees on IT needs of the business units and their understanding of each unit's activities. The right hand column of Table 6.1 indicates these differences in perceptions, with the positive differences indicating that CIOs uniformly viewed the quality of their relationships with business units more positively than did the business unit managers. It is worth noting that CIOs did not view their relationship with business units as "great." At best, they gave themselves "a moderate +" or "great –" rating.

Table 6.2 presents a comparison of business unit managers' perceptions of corporate and divisional IS groups on these same issues. There are two things that are particularly striking about these results. First, business unit managers generally rated the quality of their relations with their divisional IS group as quite high. Second, the business unit managers uniformly viewed their divisional IS group more favorably than they viewed the corporate IS group. The strength of these differences provides strong evidence supporting decentralization of IT decision making, given that one believes IS/user relations are important. Policies favoring centralized IT management strategies must account for the costs associated with potentially poorer IS/user relations.

Finally, business unit managers were asked to indicate the extent to which the line managers viewed IT as important and the extent to which they involved themselves in IT decision making (see Figures 6.13 and 6.14). The findings suggest that line managers viewed IT as being important but not too important and were only moderately involved in IT decision making.

FIGURE 6.13 **Degree to Which Line Managers View IT as Important**

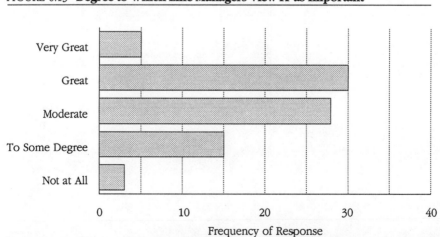

Frequency of Response

TABLE 6.2 **Business Unit View of Corporate IS Group Compared with Divisional IS Group**

	Divisional IS Group	*Corporate IS Group*	*Differences*

1. Reliability
   Quality
   Timeliness
	3.77	3.37	.40

2. Extent Commitments Carried Out	3.77	3.23	.54

3. Involvement in Planning,
   Acquiring, Proposing IT
   Services
	3.59	2.71	.88

4. Agreement on Needs,
   Opportunities,
   Goals, Priorities
	3.88	2.86	1.02

5. IS Group's Understanding
   of Operations, Strategies,
   Management Practices
	4.00	2.53	1.47

Scale: 1 = None
       3 = Moderate
       5 = Very Great

FIGURE 6.14 **Degree to Which Line Managers are Involved in IT Decision Making**

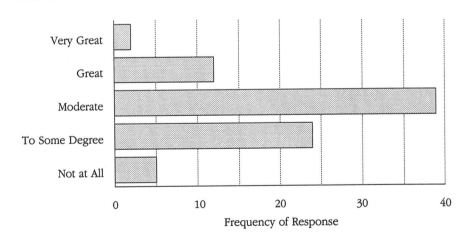

Frequency of Response

7
Survey Findings: Where Information Technology Decisions Are Made

We asked the CIO and the senior business unit executives in each company to answer another set of questions, this time regarding where a variety of IT decisions were made in their organization. These questions focused on three broad IT decision areas: long- and short-run hardware planning, long- and short-run application planning, and operations. Four groups of decision makers were examined: corporate IS management, other corporate management, business unit IS management, and other business unit management. (Divisional IS groups were referred to as "business unit IS groups" in order to specify more tightly the reponses of the business unit executives.) This chapter describes the location of IT decision responsibility among these four management groups and by type of decision.

Differences Across Management Groups

In broad terms, the CIOs and the business unit managers shared similar views of the IT decision role of each of the four management groups. Both perceived a strong or dominant role for the corporate IS group in long-run and short-run hardware decisions. Other corporate management was perceived as playing a very limited role in IT decisions. Business unit IS played a strong role in the decisions related to application development, project management, and day-to-day operations. Other business unit management played a strong role in determining applications. Also, a great deal of shared decision making was observed across the IT decisions we examined. Tables 7.1 and 7.2 summarize the responses that were given.

TABLE 7.1   **Management Roles in IT Decision Making as Perceived by Business Unit Managers**

	Corporate IS MGR	*Other Corporate Management*	*Business Unit IS MGR*	*Unit Other Management*
Long-run Decisions				
Hardware	Very Strong	Minor	Shared	Minor
Applications	Minor	Very Minor	Shared	Shared
Short-run Decisions				
Hardware	Strong	Minor	Shared	Minor
Applications	Minor	Minor	Shared	Strong
Projects	Minor	Very Minor	Strong	Shared
Operations of IS	Shared	Very Minor	Very Strong	Shared

TABLE 7.2   **Management Roles in IT Decision Making as Perceived by Corporate Chief Information Offices**

	Corporate IS MGR	*Other Corporate Management*	*Business Unit IS MGR*	*Unit Other Management*
Long-run Decisions	Strong	Minor	Shared to Strong	Minor
Hardware	Strong	Minor	Shared to Strong	Minor
Applications	Shared	Minor	Shared	Strong
Short-run Decisions				
Hardware	Strong	Minor	Shared	Minor
Applications	Minor to Shared	Minor	Shared	Strong
Projects	Shared	Minor	Strong	Shared
Operations	Strong	Minor	Strong	Shared

Role of Corporate IS Management

In assuming primary responsibility for vendors, brands, technologies, and capacities to be acquired, corporate IS management played the strongest role in hardware decisions. To the extent these decisions are shared, they tended to be shared with business unit IS managers. Corporate IS managers also played an active role in operating decisions but minor roles elsewhere.

Role of Other Corporate Management

Respondents did not view corporate management other than corporate IS management as being very involved with IT decisions. Generally, they assumed only a minor role in hardware decisions with even less involvement in application or operating decisions.

Role of Business Unit IS Management

Business unit IS management tended to share in decision making, either with the corporate IS management (on hardware decisions) or business unit management (on application decisions). They assumed primary roles for project management decisions and operating decisions.

Role of Other Business Unit Management

Non-IS business unit management appeared to play the dominant role in short-run application decisions. They tended to share decision responsibility for project management, long-run applications and, to a lesser extent, operating decisions. They played only a minor role in hardware decisions.

Implications

These findings might be summarized as follows:

— Corporate IS sets long-run direction and policy via its decisions regarding vendors and hardware capacities.

— Business unit IS identifies and implements applications and handles day-to-day operations.

— Non-IS business unit management determines which applications will be implemented.

An interesting finding is the extent to which business unit IS managers appear to share decisions with others: vertically with corporate IS, and horizontally with business unit management. It seems that business unit IS managers occupy traditional staff management slots and generally have not assumed active decision-making roles in their business units. Critical strategic IT decisions are made at the corporate IS level; critical IT application decisions are made by business unit managers. Business unit IS implements (project management decisions) and operates (day-to-day decisions). The case studies supported these conclusions and suggest such a role may become even more pervasive. Corporate IS seems committed to direction setting for technology and, in some cases, determining strategic long-run applications. At the same time, there appears to be a trend for line managers to play much more active roles in application and project management decisions. The implication of this for the business unit IS manager is unclear. However, it does seem that the business unit IS manager either must become an important part of the business unit management team by bringing skills as an information and technology manager or increasingly will become a purveyor of commodity IT services.

Comparing CIO and Business Unit Manager Responses

Table 7.3 directly compares the responses of CIOs with those of business unit managers for the questions regarding the location of IT decision-making responsibility. Three main observations arise. First, the CIOs almost uniformly viewed themselves as having a stronger role in IT decisions than the business unit managers perceived them to have. Second, CIOs viewed other corporate managers as having more responsibility for new applications, project management, and operating decisions than did the business unit managers. Finally, CIOs believed that non-IS business unit managers were more involved in long-run application decisions than did the business unit managers. Taken together, these differences suggest (1) that the business unit managers think more decentralization of IT decision making has occurred than do the CIOs; and (2) the business unit managers have a more accurate perception of what is occurring in the business units regarding IT decision making than do the CIOs.

TABLE 7.3. **CIOs' Perception of Management Decision Making Compared with Perceptions of Business Unit Managers**

	Corporate IS MGR	Other Corporate Management	Business IS MGR	Unit Other Management
Long-run Decisions				
Hardware	Stronger* Role	Same	Stronger Role	Same
Applications	Stronger Role	Stronger Role	Same	Stronger Role
Short-run Decisions				
Hardware	Same	Same	Same	Same
Applications	Slightly Stronger Role	Same	Same	Same
Projects	Stronger Role	Stronger Rate	Same	Same
Operations	Stronger Role	Stronger Role	Weaker Role	Same

*In each case the cell indicates the CIO's perception as compared with business unit managers. For this case, CIOs perceived themselves as having a stronger role in long-run hardware decisions than did business unit managers.

IT Decentralization vs.
Corporate Decentralization

While we did not directly pose a question contrasting IT decentralization with the corporate philosophy regarding decentralization, each company's CFO was asked to indicate the extent of decentralization regarding a number of operating and staff activities. In general, decentralization of IT decision making was associated with overall corporate decentralization. It appears that decentralization of IT decision making tracks with the corporate philosophy on decentralization, but the tendency is just that. The location of IT decision responsibilities may be substantively different from that of other staff or operating decision responsibilities.

Differences by Type of IT Decision

In general, we found broad differences in who makes IT decisions based on the type of decision involved. Mean responses, by both business unit managers and CIOs, for each of the questions posed are presented in Table 7.4.

Hardware Decisions

It is clear from Panel A of Table 7.4 that both business unit managers and CIOs view corporate IS management as having primary responsibility for mainframe/minicomputer vendor and capacity decisions in both the long run (three to five years) and the short run. However, corporate IS management was less dominant in making short-run vendor and capacity decisions. Corporate IS management also played a much less dominant role in making microcomputer decisions, which tended to be made by business unit IS management with substantial input from non-IS business unit managers. This appeared to hold for short- and long-run microcomputer decisions as well as for both the vendor and capacity decisions for microcomputers.

Application Decisions

Decisions about specific applications to be included in three-to-five-year IT plans generally were shared between the business unit IS management and other business unit managers. Corporate IS management and other corporate management played minor roles in these decisions. Note in Panel B of Table 7.4 that business unit managers viewed corporate management as assuming less responsibility for long-run application decisions than did the CIOs. (See cols. 2 and 6.)

TABLE 7.4   **Decision Responsibility by Type of Decision**

	Business Unit Manager Responses				Chief Information Officer Responses			
A. Hardware Decisions	IS	CO	BI	BO**	CI	CO	BI	BO**
Long-run Hardware								
Mainframe	3.3	2.0	2.8	1.9*	3.7	1.9	3.0	2.0*
Micro	2.7	2.0	3.1	2.3	2.9	2.1	3.2	2.7
Tele	3.3	2.3	2.5	2.1	3.8	2.1	2.6	2.0
Short-run Hardware								
Mainframe	3.1	2.1	2.9	2.2	3.3	2.1	3.0	2.2
Micro	2.4	1.9	3.1	2.6	2.6	2.2	3.2	2.9
Tele	3.2	2.2	2.7	2.2	3.5	1.9	2.5	2.2
B. Application Decisions								
Long-run Application								
Inbound/Outbound	2.1	1.9	2.8	3.0	2.6	2.2	2.8	2.9
Manufacturing	2.0	1.9	2.9	3.1	2.3	2.2	2.9	3.0
Marketing	2.0	2.0	2.8	3.1	2.5	2.2	3.0	3.1
Sales/Customer Ser.	2.1	1.9	2.8	3.1	2.5	2.1	3.0	3.1
Engineering/R&D	1.9	2.0	2.6	3.1	2.1	2.5	2.8	3.1
Finance/Accounting	2.4	2.5	2.8	3.0	2.5	2.7	2.9	2.9
Short-run Application								
Inbound/Outbound	2.3	2.0	2.9	2.8	2.6	2.0	2.9	3.2
Manufacturing	2.0	1.8	2.9	3.0	2.3	2.1	2.9	3.2
Marketing	2.2	2.0	2.8	3.0	2.5	2.3	2.8	3.1
Sales/Customer Ser.	2.2	1.9	2.9	3.0	2.5	2.2	2.9	3.3
Engineering/R&D	2.0	1.9	2.7	3.1	2.2	2.4	2.7	3.2
Finance/Accounting	2.4	2.4	2.9	2.8	2.5	2.6	2.9	3.2
C. Project Management Decisions								
Project Management	2.5	1.6	3.3	2.6	3.0	1.8	3.4	2.6
Essential Features and Functions	2.3	1.7	3.1	2.9	2.7	2.1	3.1	3.2
D. Operating Decisions Setting Service								
Priorities when Unforeseen Problems Arise	2.7	1.6	3.3	2.6	3.4	2.0	3.4	2.7
Overriding SOPs when Special Needs Arise	2.6	1.6	3.3	2.4	3.5	1.8	3.2	2.3
Evaluating the Quality of IT Service	2.5	2.0	3.1	2.9	3.0	2.7	3.1	3.0

* 1—Does Not Make Decision
 2—Minor Role in Decision
 3—Shares Equally in Decision
 4—Primary Role in Decision
 5—Unilaterally Makes Decision

** CI—Corporate IS Manager
 CO—Other Corporate Management
 BI—Business Unit IS Manager
 BO—Other Business Unit Management

It is also interesting to note that differences arise in decision responsibility depending on the specific application area involved. Finance/accounting decisions were much more centralized than applications involving linkages with customers or suppliers. In turn, decisions regarding engineering/R&D, manufacturing, and marketing applications appeared to be more decentralized than those involving customer or supplier linkages.

Similar patterns were observed for short-run application decisions. Business units had the principle responsibility for short run application decisions with corporate management playing a minor role. Decisions were highly shared between business unit IS management and other business unit managers with non-IS managers having the stronger role.

Project Management Decisions

Panel C of Table 7.4 provides data on the location of responsibility for project management decisions. Both corporate IS management and business unit IS management were more involved in managing IS projects than in decisions about the applications. Corporate IS shared in these decisions; business unit IS played a very strong role in these decisions. It is also clear that non-IS business unit managers, while actively involved, have not yet assumed a dominant role in either managing projects or even deciding on essential application features and functions. This was quite surprising given the sentiment often expressed in the case studies that projects were most successful when managed by prospective users.

Operating Decisions

Responses on operating decision responsibilities are reported in Panel D of Table 7.4. As we expected, business unit IS management assumed the dominant responsibility for decisions regarding the setting (or revising) of priorities when unforeseen problems or special needs arose. However, both of these decisions were shared with both corporate IS management and non-IS business unit management. As with other decisions, CIOs perceived themselves as playing a stronger role in these decisions than did their business unit managers. With these decisions, the level of disagreement was quite high.

Similar comments apply to responsibility for evaluating the IT quality, with the principle differences being a higher involvement of business unit management and a lower involvement by corporate IS management. It also interesting to note that non-IS corporate management did play a stronger role than otherwise observed in evaluating IT quality.

Measures of Shared IT Decision Making

We also examined IT decision making from a perspective of determining which decisions tended to be corporate decisions, which were shared, and which were business unit decisions. This analysis was done independent of whether primary decision responsibility lay with IS or non-IS management. Figures 7.1, 7.2, and 7.3, which illustrate our findings, are interpreted as follows:

—A decision that is fully *shared* between corporate and business unit management is represented by a value of zero.

—A decision that is largely the responsibility of corporate management, i.e., a *centralized* decision, is represented by larger positive values.

—A decision that is largely the responsibility of business unit management, i.e., a *decentralized* decision, is represented by larger negative values.

FIGURE 7.1   **Sharing of Decisions about Hardware**

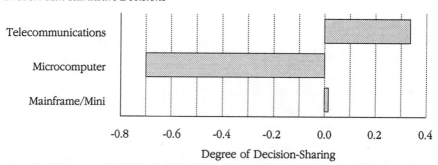

A. Long-Run Hardware Decisions

Degree of Decision-Sharing

B. Short-Run Hardware Decisions

Degree of Decision-Sharing

- = Decision made more by business unit
0 = Decision fully shared by corporate and business unit
+ = Decision made more by corporate

FIGURE 7.2   **Sharing of Decisions about Applications**

A. Long-Run Application Decisions

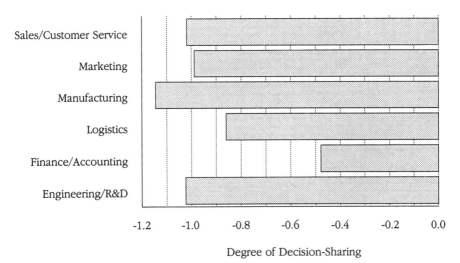

Degree of Decision-Sharing

B. Short-Run Application Decisions

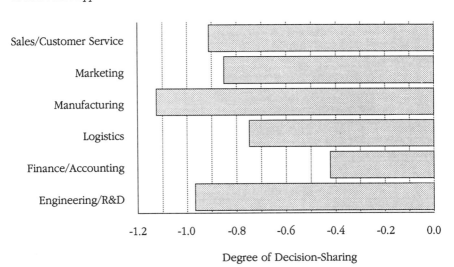

Degree of Decision-Sharing

- = Decision made more by business unit
0 = Decision fully shared by corporate and business unit
+ = Decision made more by corporate

FIGURE 7.3 **Sharing of Decisions about Projects and Operations**

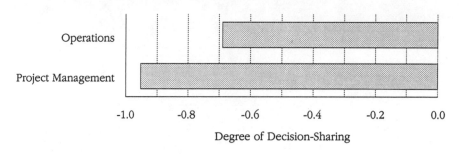

Degree of Decision-Sharing

\- = Decision made more by business unit
0 = Decision fully shared by corporate and business unit
+ = Decision made more by corporate

Figure 7.1 clearly shows that decisions about mainframe computers, mini-computers, and telecommunications—but not microcomputers—are centralized. This tendency is strongest with telecommunications and long-run hardware decisions. Short-run mainframe and minicomputer decisions tend to be shared; and microcomputer decisions, especially in the short run, are decentralized.

Figure 7.2 provides fairly strong evidence that the survey companies have moved application decisions into business units. With the exception of finance/accounting, the most frequent response is that business units have primary responsibility for both long-run and short-run application decisions. However, we must note that considerable variability exists in the response distributions.

Again, clear evidence exists to support the decentralization of project management and operating decisions to business units. (See Figure 7.3.) The response distributions document that corporate management, at most, shares in these decisions.

Comparing Business Units in the Same Company

Finally, we also examined the extent to which differences in the location of IT decision making varied across a single firm's business units. The differences that were observed were neither systematic nor larger than might be expected from perceptual differences among a firm's managers.

Conclusions

Four overall conclusions arise from these results:

1.   Hardware decisions, aside from microcomputer decisions, tend to be centralized and lie with the corporate IS group.

2. Microcomputer decisions tend to be decentralized, with primary responsibililty given to business unit IS management.

3. Long-run and short-run applications decisions are primarily handled within business units. There is considerable sharing of responsibility of applications decisions between IS and non-IS managers in these business units..

4. Project management and operating decisions tend to be decentralized with business unit IS management having primary responsibility.

The picture that emerges is one of a mixed pattern of responsibilities, where those individuals most affected by and most influential regarding specific decisions tend to take responsibility for those decisions. IT decisions that are likely to affect corporate-wide activities or are common across business units should be, and are, centralized. IT decisions that are specific to business units should be, and are, decentralized.

Still, few IT decisions are so cleanly targeted that they lie fully within corporate IS or within the business units. For example, one might conjecture, given the general acceptability of assigning a firm's operating responsibilities to line managers, that IT operating decisions would also lie with line managers. This was not the case for most of the firms we studied. Rather, IT operating decisions tended to be handled by the business unit IS group with substantial sharing in those decisions by both corporate IS management and business unit non-IS management. Our interpretation is that this reflects the fact that business unit IS groups are viewed predominantly in a manner similar to other staff functions, such as personnel or accounting. As such, they serve important organizational roles in coordinating the (at times, conflicting) interests of corporate and line management as well as facilitating line management's increasing interest in and use of IT.

8
Survey Findings: Performance Implications

The survey results also enabled us to examine the effects of different patterns of IT decision making on business unit performance, business unit reliance on IT, and the quality of relations that develop among IS personnel and users. We found only weak effects regarding business unit performance. This result is not surprising given the very large number of factors that combine to determine business performance. In fact, we would have been more surprised had we uncovered a strong effect. We did observe somewhat stronger effects regarding the degree to which business units relied on IT in supporting operating activities or carrying out strategic thrusts. Generally, a greater reliance on IT for operating activities was observed with decentralized IT decision making. Finally, there were strong associations between allocation of IT decision-making responsibility and IS group/user relations. Details on each of these findings are provided in this chapter.

Business Unit Performance

Chief financial officers in the survey companies were asked to rate their business units on the 15 performance measures given in Table 8.1. These measures, which represent performance in five areas (financial, marketing, product, manufacturing, and "other"), are not meant to be exhaustive; rather, they should be viewed as a broad spectrum of measures representing the various areas for which business units tend to be held accountable.

The CFOs rated their business units by assigning each a "grade," with "A" indicating excellent performance, with "B," "C" and "D" indicating progressively worse performance, and with "E" indicating poor performance. The CFOs were

TABLE 8.1   **Business Unit Performance Measures**

Overall Financial Performance

Operating Profits
Cash Flow from Operations
Return on Investment

Marketing Performance

Sales Revenue
Sales Growth
Market Share
Market Development

Product Performance

Product Development
Product Quality
Service Quality

Manufacturing Performance

Process Improvement
Productivity
Cost Control

Other

Personnel Development
Political/Public Affairs

asked to indicate "not applicable" for those measures that did not apply to a particular business unit.

Corporate versus Business Unit

As described in Chapter 7, long-run IT decisions tended to be retained at corporate and short-run IT decisions tended to be delegated to business units. Still, considerable variation was observed across the survey companies. The observed relations between the decision responsibility responses and the performance measures are summarized in Table 8.2. While we did not observe any strong relationships, we did find two persistent relations that are interesting. First, marketing and product performance were better when short-run IT decisions, particularly those associated with applications and project management, were decentralized to business units. Second, manufacturing performance was better when long-run hardware and applications decisions were centralized.

It is difficult to draw definitive conclusions about these observed relationships for at least two reasons. First, CFOs were asked to select for participation in the study the three business units that differed primarily on performance (high,

TABLE 8.2 **Business Unit Performance and Allocation of IT Decision Making Between Corporate and Business Unit**

	Financial Performance	*Marketing Performance*	*Product Performance*	*Manufacturing Performance Cost/Productivity*
Long-run Decisions				
Hardware	No Relation	No Relation	No Relation	Better When Centralized
Applications	No Relation	No Relation	No Relation	Better When Centralized
Short-run Decisions				
Hardware	No Relation	Slightly Better When Micro Decisions Decentralized	No Relation	No Relation
Applications	No Relation	Better When Decentralized	Better When Decentralized	Better Cost Control When Decentralized
Project Management	No Relation	Better When Decentralized	Better When Decentralized	No Relation
Operations	No Relation	No Relation	No Relation	No Relation

medium, and low performers). Because both the survey data and the case studies indicate a strong consistency across business units within each company in the assignment of IT decision responsibility, strong associations between performance and IT decision making are less likely to show up. Second, the observed relationships between decentralization and marketing and product performance may be the result of a number of possible reasons other than those postulated. Two alternative explanations, which are consistent with current trends toward decentralization in marketing-driven firms, are:

1. Senior management may simply be more willing to delegate more IT decisions to business units that are performing well.

2. Marketing and product performance may simply be greater when the general management decision-making environment (including IT decisions) is more decentralized.

Similar alternative arguments could likewise be proposed for the relationship between observed centralization of long-run hardware and application decisions and better manufacturing performance.

Business Unit IS versus Business Unit Non-IS Managers

It was our expectation that there would be more variability across the survey companies in how business units chose to carry out IT decision making than would be observed in the corporate versus business unit comparison. As a result, we expected to find potentially stronger relations for business unit performance and the apportionment of IT decision making between business unit IS and other business unit managers. This expectation held true. (See Table 8.3.)

TABLE 8.3   **Business Unit Performance and Allocation of IT Decision Making Between IS Managers and Other Managers at the Business Unit Level**

	Financial Performance	*Marketing Performance*	*Product Performance*	*Manufacturing Performance*
Long run				
Hardware	No Consistent Relationship	No Consistent Relationship	No Consistent Relationship	No Consistent Relationship
Applications	No Consistent Relationship	No Consistent Relationship	No Consistent Relationship	Better When Neither Involved
Short Run				
Hardware		Better When BU Manager. Involved	Better When Corp IS Makes Decision	Better When IS Group Makes Decision
Applications	Better When BU Manager Decides	Better When BU Manager Decides	Better When BU Manager Decides	Better When BU Manager Not Responsible for IT Decisions
Project Management	Better When IS Manager Decides	Better When BU Manager Decides	Better When IS Manager Decides	Better When BU Manager Not Respnsible For IT Decisions
Operations	No Consistent Relationship	Better When BU Manager Not Involved	Better When BU Manager Not Involved	Better When BU Manager Not Responsible For IT Decisions

Two outcomes of this analysis are important. First, no relationships were observed for long-run IT decisions. If anything, performance seemed to be better when *neither* business unit IS nor non-IS business unit managers were responsible for such decisions. A number of consistent relations was found with short-run IT decision making:

— Better performance generally occurs when business unit non-IS managers are responsible for short-run applications decisions.

— Better performance generally occurs when business unit IS managers are responsible for project management and operations decisions.

— Better manufacturing performance generally occurs when business unit non-IS managers are not responsible for short-run IT decisions.

Summary

Given the weakness of the observed relations, the discussion that follows should be viewed as tentative and preliminary rather than definitive. Generally, better performing business units have delegated decision responsibility for short-run applications to users. This is consistent with the results of the case studies that overwhelmingly supported the notion that successful IT applications are user-driven. However, it appears that in certain areas better performing business units have retained some decision responsibilities in either the corporate IS group or the business unit IS group. Specifically, business units with better performance in the area of manufacturing productivity/cost tended to have retained long-run IS decision responsibility at corporate and short-run IS decision responsibility in the business unit IS group or corporate IS group. In addition, better performing business units tended to retain responsibility for IT project management and operations in the business unit IS group. These findings were not consistent with the case study results. Still, all of the observed relationships are consistent with the notion expressed in Chapter 7 that IT decision-making responsibility should reside with those managers best able to deal with the decision issues to be resolved. A question that obviously remains unanswered is the extent to which better performing business units will continue to divide IT decision-making responsibility along such lines as line managers become both more knowledgable about IT and more confident in their use of IT and as the technology itself becomes more accessible to non-technical users.

Reliance on IT

The findings described in Chapter 6 indicated that the business units in the survey companies were much more likely to rely on IT for supporting line or staff activities than for strategic thrusts. Overall, however, we found that business units tended to rely more on IT (for line, staff, and strategic applications) when IT decision making was decentralized to the business units. Further, our results indicate that higher reliance on IT was linked to greater applications decision responsibilities by non-IS business unit managers and to greater hardware, project, and operating decision responsibilities by business unit IS managers.

Corporate versus Business Unit

Table 8.4 gives results of our examination of differences in the degree of reliance on IT based on whether specific IT decisions were the responsibility of corporate managers or business unit managers. Three observations are noteworthy. First, there was a relatively strong tendency for business units to rely more on IT to support line operations when IT decisions were delegated to business units. The results are rather weak for long-run IT decisions but strong and consistent for short-run IT decisions. Second, there was little relationship between where IT decisions were made and reliance on IT to support staff functions. Finally, business units tended to rely more on IT in order to accomplish strategic activities when IT decisions were delegated to business units. The data support at least a tentative conclusion that moving IT decision responsibility into business units is consistent with managers making greater use of IT in carrying out their operating and strategic activities.

TABLE 8.4   **Reliance on IT and Allocation of IT Decision Making Between Corporate and Business Units**

Reliance on IT For:	*Line Operations*	*Staff Functions*	*Strategy*
Long-run Decisions:			
Hardware	Slightly Greater When Decentralized	No Relation	No Relation
Applications	Greater When Decentralized	No Relation	Greater When Decentralized
Short-run Decisions			
Hardware	Much Greater When Decentralized	No Relation	Much Greater When Decentralized
Applications	Greater When Decentralized	No Relation	Greater When Decentralized
Project Management	Greater When Decentralized	No Relation	No Relation
IS Operations	Much Greater When Decentralized	Greater When Decentralized	Greater When Decentralized

Business Unit IS versus Business Unit Non-IS Managers

Our analysis also examined the differences in reliance on IT at the business unit level based on whether IT decision responsibilities lay with business unit IS managers or business unit non-IS managers. Results are given in Table 8.5. Interestingly, the results indicate that the benefits to be realized from decentralizing IT decisions to business units do not necessarily imply delegation of these decisions to line managers.

TABLE 8.5 **Reliance on IT and Allocation of IT Decision Making Between IS Managers and Other Managers at the Business Unit Level**

Reliance on IT For:	*Line Operations*	*Staff Functions*	*Strategy*
Long-run Decisions:			
Hardware	Greater When IS Responsible	No Consistent Relationship	Greater when IS Responsible
Application	No Consistent Relationship	No Consistent Relationship	Greater When Both Involved
Short-run Decisions:			
Hardware	Greater When Both Involved	No Relationship	Much Greater When IS Decides
Applications	Greater Reliance When Non-IS Managers Involved	No Relationship	Greater When Shared at BU Level
Project Management	No Relationship	No Relationship	Greater When IS Responsible
IS Operations	Greater When IS Responsible Greater When Non-IS Managers Involved in Evaluations of IT	Greater When IS Responsible	Greater When IS Responsible

Following are the main themes evident from Table 8.5.

— As with the prior analysis, few relations exist between decentralization of IT decision making and staff reliance on IT.

— More reliance on IT in supporting line operations and strategy was seen when business unit IS managers were responsible for long-run hardware decisions.

— More reliance on IT in supporting line operations was seen when business unit non-IS managers were responsible for short-run applications decisions.

— More reliance on IT in supporting strategy was seen when both business unit IS and business unit non-IS managers were responsible for applications decisions.

— More reliance on IT in supporting strategy was seen when business unit IS managers were responible for hardware, project management, and operations decisions.

— More reliance on IT in supporting line operations, staff functions, and strategy was seen when business unit IS managers were responsible for operations.

Summary

The general lack of relations regarding the use of IT in support of staff functions was initially puzzling, but on reflection this situation seemed quite reasonable. Staff organization and reporting relationships often vary significantly from one organization to another. In some organizations, staff functions may report directly to corporate staff; hence, they would be expected to receive their IT support from this corporate level. In other organizations, staff functions may report directly to business unit management with their IT support coming from business unit IS groups. Such relationships are most likely independent of a firm's overall pattern of IT decision making.

Overall, these findings are consistent with those from the case studies. Business units tend to rely more on IT when line managers are more involved in IT applications decisions and when business unit IS assumes primary responsibility for short-run hardware and operating decisions.

IS/User Relations

As presented in Chapter 6, business unit managers generally viewed IT products and services received from business unit IS groups to be higher quality, more reliable, and more timely than IT products and services received from the corporate IS group. Such perceptions held regardless of the pattern of IT decision-making responsibility between corporate and business units. Business unit managers also viewed business unit IS groups as carrying out their commitments to a greater extent than corporate IS groups. Again, this tended to be true regardless of the pattern of IT decision making. It is noteworthy, however, that business unit managers viewed corporate IS more favorably with respect to carrying out their commitments when applications, project, and operating decisions were delegated to the business unit.

Involvement in Business Unit IS Activities

Business unit managers believed that business unit IS groups were much more involved in proposing, planning, and acquiring new IT products and services than were corporate IS groups regardless of the pattern of IT decision making. Not surprisingly, a strong association existed between centralized IT decision making and increased corporate IS involvement as well as between assignment of IT decision responsibility to business units and business unit IS group involvement. Greater decision responsibility does breed at least a perception of greater involvement.

A few differences did arise regarding specific IT decisions. First, the perceived involvement of corporate IS was strongest when both long- and short-run hardware decisions were made at the corporate level. Second, the perceived involvement of business unit IS was strongest when application, project management, and operating decisions were made at the business unit. The relative strengths of these relationships add additional evidence about the potential "natural roles" of the respective IS groups in delivering IT products and services.

Agreement on Business Unit Goals, Needs, and Priorities

The corporate IS group was perceived to be much less attuned to the needs of business units than were business unit IS groups. However, corporate IS groups were viewed as more in agreement when IT decisions were centralized. Business unit IS groups were regarded as agreeing with business unit management independent of the pattern of IT decision making.

Similar statements apply to business unit managers' perception of how well the respective IS groups understand their business activities. Generally, business unit IS groups were perceived as having a high level of understanding of the business units' operations, strategies, and management practices. Again, this perception held independent of where IS decisions were made. Corporate IS groups, on the other hand, were perceived as having only a moderate level of understanding. However, their understanding of the business unit was perceived to be higher with greater IT decision centralization.

Line Manager Involvement in IS Activities

On average, the responding business unit managers indicated that their line managers viewed IT as being only moderately important to their business activities and personal performance. This perceived importance of IT did increase, however, with greater decentralization of IT decision making.

The business unit managers also were also asked to indicate the level of involvement of line managers in proposing, planning, or acquiring new IT products and services. On average, this involvement was viewed as being limited. Again, however, line manager involvement in IS activities did increase with greater decentralization of IT decision making.

Summary

The implicit assumption in examining the existence of linkages between patterns of IT decision making and IS/user relationships is that the overall quality of these relations will affect both the quality of new applications and their acceptability to users. The case studies provided strong evidence that IS managers believe the quality of their relationships with users, their understanding of the business unit, and the involvement of non-IS managers are critical to the success of new applications. To the extent this assumption (and the views of the case study IS managers) is true, better IT decisions and more effective IT applications should occur when IS/user relationships are stronger. The results of this study indicate that business unit IS groups are more likely to develop the desired relationships with users, regardless of the pattern of IT decision making. The results also support the notion that many of these relationships improve as specific IT decision responsibilities, for example, application, project management, and operating decisions, move from corporate to the business units.

Conclusion

This chapter examined the associations between the pattern of IT decision making and business unit performance, IT reliance, and IS/user relations. The results do provide IT management guidelines. However, in all cases, these conclusions must be viewed as tentative. Correlation analysis was used, and this kind of analysis does not establish causality. For example, we are not able to determine whether decentralization promotes better performance or whether better performance promotes decentralization. Alternatively, better performance and greater decentralization both may result from other factors not included in this study. However, the relationships found in the survey data are quite consistent, and the results are similar in most instances to those observed in the case studies.

The results support three broad prescriptions. First, certain IT decisions, such as long-run hardware and long-run applications decisions, should be retained in the corporate IS group when technology issues become paramount and when the potential to exploit common or joint applications is high. A good example might be that of advanced manufacturing systems, which involve complex technologies and whose implementation is often similar across a firm's business units. Second, the results support delegating short-run application decisions, (e.g., identifying and prioritizing those applications to be implemented as well as determining essential features and functions) to users. This may also prove beneficial for certain hardware decisions, particularly those associated with microcomputers. Third, the results suggest that the business unit IS group should hold primary responsibility for short-run hardware decisions, application decisions that are common across the business unit (e.g., manufacturing systems), project management decisions, and operating decisions. However, as illuminated by the case studies, such prescriptions must be moderated by factors such as organizational history, the philosophy of the organization about decentralization, the nature of the business, and the size of the organization.

9
Case Study Descriptions

Each case description begins with a discussion of the case setting. In order to facilitate comparison, corporate background information is provided first, followed by, respectively, information on each corporation's information services background, pattern of IT decision making, differences among business units regarding this pattern, the rationale behind the pattern, and the corporation's "critical success factors" for IT use.

Corporation A

Corporation A (CORP-A) is a large industrial company with about $3.25 billion in sales. It has four principle lines of business organized into operating groups, including a large, high market share basic manufacturing business (CORP-A is the largest producer in the industry), a commodity business in which they seek to be a low-cost producer, a very profitable business in which they seek to be a niche marketer of specialty items, and a small high-technology, high-growth business. CORP-A is a classic cyclical company tied to the automotive and construction industries for much of its revenues.

CORP-A has a history of good performance, dominant market shares in its core businesses, and highly profitable niche operations. It is recognized as an industry leader with a set of well defined strategies. These strategies have focused on international growth, cost reductions in commodity lines, and niche marketing of specialty items. The evidence supports a conclusion that they are achieving success in each of these areas.

Information Services Background

CORP-A is organized into four operating groups with up to 16 business units in each group. Corporate policy for 20 years has been to give strong autonomy to each group. Management of IS services at CORP-A matches this philosophy. The corporate IS unit plays a significant role in setting directions, but group-level IS units report to group-level management with only dotted-line reporting to corporate IS. At the business unit level, IS reports to group-level IS management. However, there are some plant-level IS units that report to plant managers. Thus the reporting relationships vary within operating groups and business units.

It was apparent that there was a trend at CORP-A toward carefully coordinating shared or common applications at the corporate IS group level in order to control cost and redundancy. On the other hand, there was also a trend toward assigning and physically moving IS group personnel out to the users. Woven throughout the two apparently divergent trends is a heavy use of IS steering committees at corporate, operating group, and business unit levels. In addition, new application projects are overseen by steering committees. Steering committees are composed of both line and IS personnel.

As can be seen from Table 9.1, CORP-A has been and and continues to be a higher than average user of information technology. Of particular interest are observations that:

1.   They are very early adopters of new IT, being among the earliest of the companies in our sample in installing data base management systems, external data services, a data base administrator and microcomputers.

2.   Although they are very early adopters, they are only slightly above average in their use of IT to support operations and strategies.

3.   The corporate IS head count reflects the staff in a very large data center that handles large-volume computing on a contract basis with operating groups. The data center is accountable as a pure profit center.

4.   Difficulty in obtaining accurate counts on LANs, number of microcomputers in the enterprise and total IS head count reflects the size, degree of decentralization, and mixed organizational reporting responsibilities at CORP-A.

Distribution of IT Decision Making

The distribution of IT decisions at CORP-A is summarized in Table 9.2. The dominant feature of CORP-A's IT management strategy is its heavy use of steering committees. They are used extensively for planning, evaluating, prioritizing, and approving. For example, there is a very senior-level committee on Information Resource Management, which includes the senior vice-president for technology and the operating group managers, that approves the IS strategic plan as well as oversees the corporate IS committee. The corporate IS committee includes the corporate IS director and each of the operating group IS directors. They meet

TABLE 9.1   **CORP-A's IT Environment**

Very early adopter
Good use of IT in support of operations
Moderate-to-good use of IT in support of strategies
Above average sophistication

Production data in DBMS:	50%
Interactive applications:	80%
Fourth-generation language applications:	20%
Microcomputers linked by LANSs	N/A
Number of mainframes/minis:	18
Number of micros:	N/A
Corporate IS head count:	81
Divisional IS head count:	N/A

monthly to review strategy and technology and to address planning and personnel issues. Similar committees function at the operating group level and at the business unit level. Thus, CORP-A has a very high degree of coordination and planning despite an organization philosophy and structure that is designed to give substantial autonomy to operating units.

TABLE 9.2   **CORP-A's IT Decision-Making Pattern**

Corporate IS	Divisional IS	Line Management
	GROUP LEVEL	
* Corporate IT strategic planning	* Sets group IT standards	* Sets priorities
* Plans, develops, and corporate systems	* Develops, manages, and manages, and operates group-wide applications	* Determines needs
* Corporate-wide IT standards	* Group IT planning	* Project management for small projects
* Corporate-wide IT services		* IT planning
* IT oversight	BUSINESS UNIT LEVEL	
	* IT planning	
	* Develops and manages buiness unit applications	

As a result, the corporate IS group plays a strong role in decisions that are significant for the corporation as a whole, or where there is sharing of a data base. They view their role as threefold. First, they plan and set IT directions for the corporation. This includes, for example, setting policy for data and voice communications worldwide. Second, they have responsibility for a large-scale data center that operates as a profit center. They do large-scale on-line transaction processing for users in the operating groups. They provide service, processing capacity, and data security. They do not provide the software. Third, they have a development group that services corporate staff departments and consults with operating groups or business units on a fee basis.

The group level IS staff members play a role similar to the corporate group except at the operating group and business unit levels. They are responsible for planning, setting standards, shared services, and providing technical support. For hardware decisions, they do the analysis and make recommendations. For software, they develop it only if it is common across business units. However, business unit IS directors report to the group IS manager and many are not located in the business units.

At the business unit level, they have an IS director or IS teams depending on the size of the business unit. Projects are managed and small local system or microcomputer planning is done at the business unit level. At all levels, the IS groups tend to retain decision responsibility for hardware decisions, be they vendor- or capacity-related, with relatively little decision sharing with users. The IS groups assume similar responsibility for operations.

Group and business unit management share in decisions about long-range applications plans as well as current projects. Similarly, they share in project management. At the business unit level, they also play a heavy role in evaluating IS personnel and the quality of IS services. They have final decision authority for new applications. The IS group may propose solutions, but it is up to business unit managers to decide if the project aligns with their business strategy and is worth continuing.

Differences Across Divisions

The philosophy of autonomy and decentralization does not differ substantially across operating groups. However, there are differences in the degree of autonomy granted to business unit IS personnel. In some cases, IS personnel have physically moved to business units or plants. In those cases, they exercise considerably more autonomy in both short- and long-run decisions than IS personnel assigned to business units but housed in operating group headquarters. The general view among IS directors is that the people in the units or plants are able to be much more responsive and are more attuned to business needs. Decentralization also has allowed them to function better as a member of the business unit management team. The cost has been interruption and lower efficiency. They view decisions to decentralize in terms of responsiveness and efficiency trade-offs. The consensus is that the trend to move IS personnel into business units will continue.

There were also some differences in the degree of involvement of business unit managers in long-run and short-run decisions. Managers clearly perceived themselves as sharing less than equally in application decisions in some units, while sharing equally in others. In some cases, the differences may be strictly perceptual. In others, they reflect the implementation of corporate policies or use of the corporate data center in one group but not in another.

Rationale

CORP-A seeks to balance the benefits of autonomy with the efficiencies provided by common technologies. On balance, however, they appear to be moving toward more autonomy. Following are the principle reasons cited:

1. Pushing IT decisions out to plants or business units increases non-IS management involvement.

2. Decentralization leads to better knowledge of business unit strategy and operations by IS managers. The implicit assumption, of course, is that this leads to better applications.

3. Assignment of IS personnel to business units increases the role of IS managers in operating, tactical, and strategic decisions.

4. Decentralization makes the IS role less adversarial and more positive.

5. Some of the reduced efficiency and redundancy that results from decentralization can be offset by greater coordination of inter- and intra-group activities. Steering committees are one means of accomplishing the sought-after coordination. Another is formalized IT plans and policies for common technology and applications from both corporate IS and the operating group IS functions.

Critical Success Factors

Table 9.3 lists those factors that CORP-A believes are most critical in successfully introducing IT applications. They fall into four main categories:

1. Those reflecting the capabilities of the IS staff (Factors 1 and 2).
2. Those associated with organizational strategies for IT management (Factors 3-5).
3. Those reflecting the capabilities of line management (Factor 6).
4. Those typical of a supportive organizational environment (Factor 7).

TABLE 9.3 **CORP-A's Critical Success Factors**

1. IS staff understands business issues and requirements
2. Highly qualified IS personnel
3. Careful IT planning
4. Early IT deliverables
5. Making open-ended technical decisions
6. User champions
7. Senior management support for IT strategic planning

A recurring theme throughout discussions of critical success factors was the requirement that new applications be supportive of business strategies. Also, because of heavy pressure for cost reductions, careful planning and implementation were critical for achieving the goals promised for an application. Both of these factors support the need for closer interaction and communication between IS personnel and users and a higher level of knowledge, by each, of the others' activities.

Corporation B

Corporation B (CORP-B) is a very successful, large (roughly $2.5 billion in sales) chemicals firm that has transformed itself in the past ten years from one that competed primarily in commodity markets to one now competing primarily in specialty markets. As might be expected, this transition drastically changed the nature of the firm's competitive environment. Put simply, CORP-B operates in a very dynamic world, where market trends must be identified and reacted to quickly and where acquisition, divestment, and joint venture activities have become the norm rather than the exception.

This transition has required that CORP-B drastically change its culture and style from one of centralization to one of decentralization. Accordingly, managerial responsibility and authority has moved lower and lower throughout this decade of change. The current managerial philosophy envisions each operating facility as self-contained. Managerial and work systems of each facility are only loosely connected.

Information Services Background

Information services at CORP-B were handled in a very centralized fashion prior to the transition described above. Few computers existed outside of corporate headquarters. Today, CORP-B has decentralized much of its IS activities and hundreds of computers exist at divisional facilities. The decentralization that has occurred can perhaps best be described as follows:

Ten years ago, IT use was led by the corporate IS group.

Five years ago, IT use was led by the divisional IS groups.

Today, IT use is led by line management with heavy involvement by the divisional IS groups and advisory support from the corporate IS group.

Five years from now, IT use is expected to continue to be led by line management but with only advisory support from the divisional IS groups and minimal, if any, support from the corporate IS group.

Even with this decentralization, a number of application areas (financial, marketing, sales) remain a corporate IS responsibility. For the most part, this is a remnant of the centralized IT decision making era rather than a reflection of current corporate policies. However, these centralized applications are being challenged by certain of the divisional IS groups, who expressed frustration with the situation.

As can be seen from Table 9.4, CORP-B has and continues to be an extensive user of information technology. Three items are particularly noteworthy:

1. While it has been quite successful in applying IT to support business operations, CORP-B has not been as successful in developing strategic information systems.

2. The centralization era seems to have provided CORP-B quite early with a sophisticated technological base.

3. The IS head counts directly reflect the decentralization of information services that has occurred.

TABLE 9.4   **CORP-B's Information Services Environment**

Very early adopter
Good IT use in support of business operations
Fair IT use in support of business strategies
High sophistication

Production data in DBMS:	80%
Interactive applications:	80%
Fourth-generation language applications:	30%
Micros linked via LANs:	20%
Number of mainframes/minis:	50
Number of micros:	2000
Corporate IS head count:	132
Divisional IS head count:	1000

Distribution of IT Decision Making

The most distinguishing feature of CORP-B's IT management strategy is the large role served by line management. Line managers are responsible for the success of the information systems used to support the business activities under their authority. Thus, they are expected to develop IT plans, identify IT needs, and manage the projects that provide the information systems to meet these needs. Table 9.5 summarizes the distribution of IT-related responsibilities across corporate IS, divisional IS, and line management.

TABLE 9.5   **CORP-B's IT Decision Making Pattern**

Corporate IS	Divisional IS	Line Management
* Sets corp IT standards	* Develops and operates IT applications	* IT planning
* Plans, develops, and operates corporate-wide applications	* Moves applications across facilities	* Manages IS projects
* IT oversight	* Determines IT strategies	* Specifies needs

Much of the IS activities that occur are handled by the divisional IS staff, who (1) determine the division's IT architecture, (2) work very closely with line managers in setting priorities and initiating projects, and (3) are deeply involved in acquiring, developing, implementing, and operating the division's information systems. Over time, however, the divisional IS staff is serving more of a technology-transfer than an application-development role.

Aside from responsibility for CORP-B's corporate-wide applications, the corporate IS group has a three-part role. First, the corporate IS group has defined an envelope (i.e., hardware, software, vendor, and telecommunication standards), within which the divisions are to operate. The divisions generally conform to these standards, but waivers can be negotiated if a strong case is made. Second, the corporate IS group specifies which applications are corporate-wide and which remain in the domain of divisions. As mentioned above, this has become an area of contention. Third, the corporate IS group approves all major IT projects. The intent here is to insure adherence to the envelope and to provide a third-party assessment of projects.

The corporate IS group had to do a considerable amount of selling for line management to buy into such a decentralized strategy. Interestingly, all interviewees seemed very satisfied with the strategy except for one issue: a concern that the corporate IS group should be playing a larger role in setting strategic IT direction.

Differences Across Divisions

Considerable consistency existed across divisions except for one division whose market was quite different from all other divisions and that traditionally had operated independently of the corporation. Because expensive, general-purpose software serves as the engine by which much of this division's work is performed, IT is a critically important resource. This has been recognized by the division's president, who has given the division's IS director (and his staff) much more responsibility for directing and controlling the division's IS activities. This philosophy is perhaps best represented by the fact that the IS director chairs the division's strategic planning committee.

One other interesting difference between divisions was whether the divisional IS director reported to a line executive or to the controller. Less line management involvement seemed to be occurring within divisions where the IS director reported to the controller.

Rationale

Three related arguments were consistently given in support of CORP-B's decentralized strategy:

1. It matched the prevailing corporate philosophy regarding centralization vs. decentralization.

2. When divisions compete in specialty markets, it is to be expected that their information needs will differ significantly. In such situations, each division must be allowed considerable autonomy.

3. In order to survive in a competitive, hostile business environment (CORP-B's expressed view of its environment), information technology management must be in the hands of line management since line managers best understand the pulse of the marketplace and the demands of customers. As expressed by one interviewee, "Our information needs are customer-driven."

Critical Success Factors

Table 9.6 lists those factors believed necessary by those interviewed for CORP-B to be successful in applying IT. These factors fall into three main categories:

1. Those reflecting the capabilities of line management (Factors 1-2).

2. Those reflecting the capabilities of the IS staff (Factors 3-5).

3. Those typical of a supportive organizational environment (Factor 6).

TABLE 9.6   **CORP-B's Critical Success Factors**

1. Line management commitment
2. Line management education
3. IS credibility
4. IS ability to respond effectively when asked
5. IS understands the business
6. Senior management support

Each of these critical success factors centers on the rather large IT responsibilities of line managers at CORP-B. A theme expressed throughout these interviews was the importance of increasing the confidence of line managers in their abilities to apply IT effectively. Such confidence grows through exposure, experience, and trust.

Corporation C

Corporation C (CORP-C) is a very successful firm holding leading positions in most of its markets. About 80 percent of its (approximately) $1.5 billion in sales is derived from consumer and industrial products that are manufactured in high-volume runs in single-purpose plants. The corporation has been active both in acquiring and divesting operating units in the past few years. A majority of the corporation's divisions are located within the same geographic region.

In the past 10 years, CORP-C has been moving to a decentralized style of corporate management in order to better tie divisional managerial and work systems to the markets within which each division competes. Most corporate services, aside from finance, accounting, and treasury, have been moved to operating units.

Information Services Background

Historically, information systems activities at CORP-C had, been handled in a relatively centralized manner. This was not attributed to a mandated corporate policy. Most, but not all, divisional managements had left responsibilities for information services to the corporate unit. Divisions located geographically distant from corporate headquarters tended to handle their own information services, as did a few located in close proximity to corporate headquarters.

Information services have followed the general corporate movement to a decentralized management style. The current corporate IS director, who directly reports to CORP-C's chief executive officer, has intensified this over the last two years. A second transition involves the managerial reporting relations for divisional IS managers. They are moving from the division's controller to the division's chief operating officer.

As can be seen from Table 9.7, CORP-C has and continues to be an extensive user of IT. Two items, however, are noteworthy:

1. While it has been quite successful in applying IT in support of business operations, CORP-C has not been as successful in developing and implementing strategic information systems.

2. The IS head counts directly reflect decentralization that has occurred with information services.

TABLE 9.7 **CORP-C's IT Environment**

Early adopter
Good IT use in support of business operations
Fair IT use in support of business strategies
Moderate sophistication

Production data in DBMS:	20%
Interactive applications	40%
Fourth-generation language applications:	10%
Micros linked via LANs:	10%
Number of mainframes/minis:	60
Number of micros:	750
Corporate IS head count:	34
Divisional IS headcount:	255

Distribution of IT Decision Making

CORP-C's divisional IS groups play the major role in managing the corporation's use of IT. Not only do they operate in an autonomous fashion *vis-a-vis* corporate IS, but they are responsible for and handle most of the IS activities that take place within the divisions. Table 9.8 summarizes the distribution of IT responsibilities across corporate IS, divisional IS, and line management.

TABLE 9.8 **CORP-C's IT Decision-Making Pattern**

Corporate IS	Divisional IS	Line Management
* Advisor to corporate and divisional IS	* IT planning	* Specifies needs
* Sets corporate IT policies and standards	* Application development	* Sets IS priorities
* IT oversight	* Operations	
* General purpose IT services		

The main role served by the corporate IS group is that of an IT consultant to both corporate management and divisional IS groups. Although corporate IS establishes policies and standards regarding vendors and technologies (to achieve corporate-wide connectivity/compatibility), such standards are viewed as guidelines rather than mandates. Most of these guidelines are followed by the divisions. While the corporate IS group must formally approve all major IT purchases, the divisional plans are rarely overridden. Finally, CORP-C attempts to leverage economies of scale wherever it is in the best interest of both the corporation and the divisions to do so. Thus, corporate IS arranges volume discounts on hardware and software and allows access by the divisions to expensive, general-purpose applications (such as publishing and graphic arts services) and technical analyses (such as investigation of alternative networking schemes).

Line management at CORP-C currently plays a fairly passive role regarding IT decision making. While it is line management's responsibility to establish divisional IT priorities and to specify information needs, divisional IS staff members play very active roles in such activities. Line management is highly involved with IS activities once divisional IT directions are set.

Differences Across Divisions

Two interesting patterns appeared to exist across CORP-C's divisions. First, greater decentralization appeared to be associated with the length of time a division had been handling its own IS activities. Second, further decentralization appeared to occur in those divisions where the divisional IS director did not report to the divisional controller. We will explore each of these patterns briefly.

One of the divisions examined had always handled its own IS activities. (This division sells a system of components to industrial markets; most other divisions sell discrete products to either industrial or consumer markets.) As a result, its managerial and work systems are quite distinct from most other divisions, and its line managers are more technically-oriented than line mangers in other divisions. The division's line managers were quite actively involved in the division's IS activities. In fact, line management handled most of the specialized applications (such as CAD/CAM) while the divisional IS staff handled core business systems (sales, distribution, customer service, etc.).

Most (10 of 13) of the divisional IS directors reported to the division's controller. There seemed to be a general consensus that line management involvement was greatest in those divisions where the divisional IS director reported to the division's general manager rather than controller. One common theme ran through the comments made about this situation: It was more difficult for the divisional IS staff to develop close, informal working relationships with line management when they were administratively linked to the controller.

Rationale

A number of forces were seen as driving CORP-C's movement of IT decision responsibilities from the corporate IS group to the divisional IS groups:

1. It matched the prevailing corporate philosophy regarding centralization vs. decentralization.

2. It is much easier to introduce or enhance applications when there is no need to consider the other divisions' concerns. As a result, the IS staff is able to respond to line manager requests in a quicker, better, more flexible manner.

3. It motivates the division's IS staff to learn more about the division's business and it educates line management on the value of IT to the business. Thus, it becomes an important step in developing a partnership between the IS staff and line management.

4. It was enabled by the decreasing costs and increasing ease-of-operation of IT. Divisions are able both to afford and operate these technologies largely without the direct support of the corporate IS group.

5. It was suggested that the corporate IS group had grown too "fat," and it was possible to reduce total IS expenses by decentralizing.

It is important to remember that, for the most part, decentralization at CORP-C stops with the divisional IS group. This was explained in two main ways. First, while line management knows where the business is going, the IS staff is seen as being in the best position to react technologically to this business direction. Second, CORP-C has had very little experience with its decentralized approach to IT management. As a result, the IS staff had not had sufficient time to build the relationships with line management necessary for line managers to become more actively involved in IT decision making. The potential advantages of a more proactive line management were observed in one division having intensive line management involvement. Their line managers have a much better understanding of the potential value of IT products and services, largely because they believe they ". . . control their own destiny and do not have to deal with a corporate bureaucracy . . ." when applying IT.

Critical Success Factors

Table 9.9 lists those factors believed necessary by those interviewed for CORP-C to be successful in applying IT. These factors fall into four main categories:

1. Those reflecting the capabilities of the IS staff (Factors 1-3).

2. Those reflecting the capabilities of line management (Factors 4 and 5).

3. Those characteristic of synergistic working relations between the IS staff and line management (Factors 6 and 7).

4. Those characteristic of a supportive organizational environment (Factors 8 and 9)

TABLE 9.9   **CORP-C's Critical Success Factors**

1. Talented IS staff
2. IS staff's ability to market the value of IT and its own abilities to line management
3. IS staff understands the business
4. Line managers understand the business value of IT, especially how IT can be applied in an offensive manner
5. Line managers possess realistic expectations of what can be achieved with IT
6. Development of a sense of partnership between IS staff and line management
7. Effective link between IS planning and business planning
8. Top management support for IT investments
9. High overall managerial performance

These critical success factors are very interesting in that (1) partnership relations are unlikely to develop until the IS staff has achieved credibility in the eyes of line management, and (2) a supportive organizational environment exists (i.e., sufficient resources are available). The consensus was that the decentralization of IT decision making was directly associated with these critical success factors.

Corporation D

Corporation D (CORP-D) is a large (sales in excess of $1 billion), manufacturer of durable goods. They operate in both domestic and international markets with manufacturing facilities in North America, South America, and Europe. They manufacture finished goods for industrial markets as well as components for other manufacturers.

CORP-D has a recent history of low profits in most of its business units. They attribute their problems to weak industrial demand and foreign competition. The corporation recently has shown overall operating losses and declining sales. It has been performing in the bottom one-third of its industry for the past three years. Some of its business units, however, are highly competitive and are showing good growth and profitability.

Information Services Background

Information services at CORP-D were highly centralized until six years ago. Corporate IS had responsibility for most IS activities aside from those associated with foreign subsidiaries, certain activities related to manufacturing (shop floor control), and purchasing. Even these manufacturing and purchasing applications, however, ran on corporate hardware. Six years ago, in part in response to a change in senior management, the IS function was decentralized. Business units are now largely responsible for all internal (to the unit) IT decisions subject only to review by corporate IS when preset spending levels are exceeded. Business unit IS groups have no formal reporting relationship with corporate IS; they report directly to business unit management. The corporate IS group now primarily serves corporate level needs and works only occasionally with business unit IS groups on a consulting basis. As a result, CORP-D is moving toward treating the IS services provided to business units by the corporate IS group as corporate overhead, that is, no direct charges assigned to the business units. This decentralization of IT decision making has remained despite the departure of the senior management that put it in place.

As can be seen in Table 9.10, CORP-D is an early adopter of IT, particular regarding DBMS and interactive applications. It also has a large number of microcomputers and interactive terminals. However, its success in using IT in support of business operations and strategies has been mixed. Three comments amplify this scenario:

1. Business units are most successful in applying IT to purchasing, manu-
    facturing, engineering, and finance/accounting. In these areas business
    unit IS and corporate management have retained a more active role in
    information system planning and development. Success in applying IT
    in marketing, sales, customer service, and personnel applications varies
    across business units. Better business performance appears either to
    result from or foster successful IT use.

2. CORP-D makes extensive use of interactive terminals in addition to
    microcomputers. Roughly half of all managers have workstations at their
    desks.

3. The IS head counts reflect the decentralization which has occurred over
    the past six years.

TABLE 9.10   **CORP-D's IT Environment**

Early adopter of most information technologies
Mixed use of IT in support of business operations
Better than average use of IT in support of business strategies
High sophistication

Production data in DBMS:	90%
Interactive applications:	90%
Fourth-generation language applications:	10%
Micros linked by LANs:	20%
Number of mainframes/minis:	8
Number of micros:	1000
Corporate IS head count:	38
Divisional IS head count:	312

Distribution of IT Decision Making

The most striking characteristic of CORP-D's strategy regarding IT decision making is the lack of involvement of corporate IS in business unit IT decisions. Corporate IS plays a minor role in hardware decisions and has virtually no formal role in other decisions affecting business unit IS. Further, business unit IS groups assume dominant decision responsibility only for hardware-related decisions. Table 9.11 summarizes CORP-D's pattern of IT decision making.

TABLE 9.11   **CORP-D's IT Decision Making Pattern**

Corporate IS	Business Unit IS	Line Management
* Plans, develops, and operates corporate systems	* IT planning for mainframe and minis	* Initiates projects
* Advisory on hardware vendor and capacity	* Application development	* Specifies needs
* IT oversight	* Operations	* Sets priorities
	* Project management	* IT planning for micros and telecommunications

Line management at CORP-D plays an active role in managing IT. Business unit IS groups report to business unit management. Divisions within units typically have their own mainframe if size can justify it, and IS activities are then fully managed at the division level. Line and staff managers decide on plans for end-user computing expenditures, such as microcomputer and LANs as part of their annual plans. Business unit IS groups provide vendor hardware and software standards. Further, line management is responsible for identifying applications, deciding on requirements and, in some units, testing the software once it is written or acquired.

Differences Across Divisions

There is little difference in IT decision making across business units. However, there are differences in business unit culture, which seem to affect the extent of decentralization. IT decision-making decentralization is most extensive in those units that had been acquired by CORP-D and those with foreign subsidiaries, which have always been decentralized. The most decentralized division has pushed mainframe/minicomputer hardware decisions and new IT application project management out to the level of the user. Interestingly, this division is also the most successful of CORP-D's business units in applying IT to support business operations and business strategies. The corporate IS group plays the same role across all business units (i.e., advice or guidance on hardware decisions and consulting on other decisions).

Rationale

CORP-D's rationale for decentralizing IT responsibilities to business units is quite simple. Business unit IS personnel and business unit line managers are in a much better position to determine their IT requirements than is the corporate IS group. Decentralization carried to the level of the user provides both faster response and a better solution. This is particularly the case with CORP-D, as its divisions engage in distinctly different business activities.

An additional motivation for decentralization is a belief by the corporate IS group that centralization was getting in the way of IS/user relationships. Not only did business units resent corporate IS telling them what to do, but there was considerable red tape and a bureaucracy that slowed and discouraged new projects. In sum, business unit managements felt that corporate IS no longer understood their increasingly complex businesses. With the shift of all business unit IS personnel to the business units and with corporate IS providing little resistance to the acquisition and deployment of IT, the business units were made more accountable for both their IT use and business results.

The timing of the decentralization was based on three factors. First, the change in corporate management philosophy that took place six years ago resulted in most business functions in the company being decentralized, except for financial decisions and certain manufacturing decisions common across units. Second, improvements and cost reductions in hardware and software made such a move economically feasible. Third, CORP-D was becoming increasingly a multi-product, multi-activity organization.

Critical Success Factors

Table 9.12 summarizes those factors that individuals interviewed at CORP-D believed were essential for successful application of IT. The factors fall into five main categories:

1. Those reflecting the capabilities of the IS staff (Factors 1 and 2).

2. Those characteristic of synergistic working relations between the IS staff and line management (Factor 3-5).

3. Those reflecting the capabilities of line management (Factor 6).

4. Those typical of a supportive organizational environment (Factor 7).

5. Those associated with organizational strategies for IT management (Factor 8).

Underlying all but two of these factors is the need for joint understanding of IT and the business by both IS personnel and line managers. This reflects the heavy emphasis at CORP-D on participation by users in initiating applications and evaluating and deciding on the final product. Successful joint understanding contributes to the other two factors, momentum and a climate of innovation.

TABLE 9.12   **CORP-D's Critical Success Factors**

1. Talented IS staff
2. Understanding of business by IS staff
3. Ability of IS staff to provide important information to management
4. Momentum from prior IT success breeds new applications
5. Integration of applications with operations
6. Line management that understands potential of IT
7. Organizational philosophy and culture supportive of introduction of new technology
8. IT decision making located at a level and place where information products and services are being used

Corporation E

Corporation E (CORP-E), a successful medium-sized firm (roughly $600 million in sales) in the food processing industry, was initially formed under the auspices of a growers' cooperative. While some of CORP-E's growth has been internal, much is attributed to its policy of acquiring regional food companies. It is perhaps best described today as a relatively loose confederation of regional divisions in very similar lines of business, all of which operate quite autonomously and are characterized by differing management philosophies, styles, and systems.

Two aspects of CORP-E's overall management philosophy are particularly important to this analysis:

1. Perhaps because of its formation by a growers' cooperative, CORP-E has very lean managerial staffs at both corporate and divisional levels.

2. Perhaps because of its growth policy of acquiring strong regional food companies, operating decisions are made within divisions.

Over time, however, there has been a movement to more active corporate-level involvement in many service functions (such as finance, cash management, marketing and human resources) in order to promote more consistency across divisions and to better leverage capital investments. No such movement has occurred, however, with information services.

Information Services Background

Information systems activities at CORP-E have always been handled fully within the divisions. In fact, there has never been a corporate IS group. While outside consultants periodically assess the continued viability of these policies, there has never been any corporate pressure to change these information technology management practices. The strength of this divisional autonomy is perhaps best seen in that there is little (hardware/software) compatibility or managerial interaction across divisional IS groups.

As can be seen from Table 9.13, CORP-E has and continues to be an active user of IT. Three items, however, are noteworthy:

1. While CORP-E has been quite successful in applying IT to support business operations, general agreement exists that the corporation has not aggressively pursued the development and implementation of strategic information systems.

2. CORP-E is not applying newer, sophisticated IT. Interviewees supported such an observation and explained that a likely cause was the lack of corporate-wide direction and funding.

3. The very small corporate IS head count (the positions indicated represent programming support for corporate-level activities) directly reflects the lack of a corporate IS group.

TABLE 9.13   **CORP-E's IT Environment**

Mid-range adopter
Very good IT use in support of business operations
Moderate IT use in support of business strategies
Low sophistication

Production data in DBMS:	30%
Interactive applications:	30%
Fourth-generation language applications:	0%
Micros linked via LANs:	0%
Number of mainframes/minis:	9
Number of micros:	102
Corporate IS head count:	3
Divisional IS head count:	43

Distribution of IT Decision Making

CORP-E's divisional IS groups play the dominant role in managing the corporation's use of IT. Not only do they operate autonomously (there being no corporate information services group), but they significantly influence divisional IS plans and priorities. Table 9.14 summarizes the distribution of IT decision making across corporate IS, divisional IS, and line management.

TABLE 9.14   **CORP-E's IT Decision Making Pattern**

Corporate IS	Divisional IS	Line Management
None	* Directs and controls most IT activities	* Initiates projects
		* Sets priorities
		* Specifies needs

Line management at CORP-E currently plays a fairly active role in initiating IS activities but a minimal role otherwise. Divisional IS directors exert considerable influence in the initiation of IS activities through their active participation on key divisional committees.

Differences Across Divisions

In one division, line managers not only initiate IS activities but are expected to manage the projects undertaken by the divisional IS staff. The IS group in this division serves more of a pure support role than the other divisional IS groups. This difference was explained as the management philosophy of the division's IS director and did not represent a shift in managerial philosophy by either corporate or divisional officers. The division's prior IS director operated in a fashion similar to the other divisions.

Rationale

A number of forces were seen as driving CORP-E's relatively stable pattern of IT decision responsibilities:

1. The current situation is largely explained by CORP-E's acquisition program. When CORP-E was initially formed, one business operation had a very good IS group that began to serve the entire firm. When the acquisition program began, this IS group could not expand to handle its own IS activities as well as those of the acquired business. Thus, the IS group of the acquired business was kept intact. Following a similar pattern, each of the acquired businesses has retained its own information systems and its own IS group.

2. While it is recognized that CORP-E is paying a price for its highly divisionalized IT management strategy (the inability to move applications from one division to another or to leverage IT learning and investments across divisions), the advantages of each division "tailoring" its applications and the perceived costs of standardization lead most managers to conclude that movement toward any centralization would do more harm than good.

3. The preference for a lean managerial structure is believed to prevent line managers from taking a more active role in IT decision making.

Interestingly, this pattern does not match the prevailing corporate movement toward some centralization of corporate-wide services. The cost of standardization is generally viewed as being too great at this late date.

Critical Success Factors

Table 9.15 lists those factors believed necessarry by those interviewed for CORP-E to be successful in applying IT. These factors fall into three main categories:

1. Those reflecting the capabilities of the IS staff (Factors 1-3).

2. Those reflecting the capabilities of line management (Factors 4-5).

3. Those representing the constraints of the organization's financial environment (Factors 6-7).

Such critical success factors characterize this environment as one where the IS staff (here, the divisional IS staffs) is driving the firm's IS activities via a reactive mode of behavior.

TABLE 9.15 **CORP-E's Critical Success Factors**

1. IS credibility
2. IS responsiveness to users
3. IS positioned to respond to user requests
4. Line management commitment to IT use
5. Existence of user champions
6. Cost/benefit justification exists
7. Adequacy of IS budget

Corporation F

Corporation F (CORP-F) is a relatively small energy company with $420 million in sales. It has a number of small subsidiaries, all of which are located in the same geographic area. All management personnel are housed under the same roof. Ninety-five percent of their revenues are generated by a single category of product.

The industry in which they operate has struggled to remain profitable over the past few years. However, CORP-F has been able to generate a very reasonable return on assets and has outperformed 90 percent of the firms in its industry. In addition, it has experienced some limited growth while most of the industry has remained stagnant or shrunk.

Overall, CORP-F is highly centralized. Subsidiaries engage in day-to-day operations, but most decisions are made at the corporate level.

Information Services Background

Prior to 1981, CORP-F used an IBM System 3 to handle its basic data processing activities. In 1981, the company installed Hewlett-Packard (HP) hardware with a large number of interactive terminals. At that time, they formed committees of users (most of whom had only manual systems) to "blue sky" potential applications over a six-month time period. A second committee was formed to set development priorities with highest priority assigned to replacing existing systems, intermediate priority to other basic business applications, and lowest priority to those blue sky applications that received the lowest initial priority. Currently, there is no new-application backlog, blue sky or otherwise.

CORP-F continues to operate the HP system with all IS personnel housed at corporate headquarters. They have a very small corporate IS group (seven people) and do not envision significant expansion in the foreseeable future. No full-time IS personnel reside elsewhere in the corporation.

TABLE 9.16   **CORP-F'S IT Environment**

Mixed (early and late) adoption history
Very good IT use in support of business operations
Limited IT use in support of business strategies
High sophistication

Production data in DBMS:	90%
Interactive applications:	90%
Fourth-generation language applications:	100%
Micros linked by LANs:	0%
Number of mainframes:	3
Number of micros:	0
Corporate IS head count:	7
Divisional IS head count:	0

As can be seen in Table 9.16, CORP-F is a very sophisticated user of IT. Most of its applications are interactive and it makes heavy use of fourth-generation languages. Several other items are noteworthy:

1. CORP-F was relatively late in adopting IT compared with other firms in our sample but vaulted ahead of most of these firms in terms of sophistication with the installation of its HP system in 1981.

2. It has not yet felt the need to install microcomputers.

3. It has been very successful in applying IT to support important line and staff operations.

4. CORP-F has had very limited success in applying IT to support business strategies.

5. The IS head count is exceptionally low. However, it does not reflect the sizable number of part-time application developers in line and staff departments, who spend up to 20 percent of their time developing applications via a fourth-generation language. In a real sense, the IS head count reflects neither the human resources committed to IS activities nor the extent to which IT decision making has been decentralized.

Distribution of IT Decision Making

CORP-F's IS function is highly centralized from a traditional perspective despite the small size of the corporate IS group. However, as inferred above and as seen from Table 9.17, CORP-F is not as centralized as might first appear. The corporate IS group makes vendor and capacity decisions as well as project management decisions for nonuser developed applications and is responsible for IT operations. Line (and staff) managers, however, are responsible for initiating applications. In some cases, application development occurs without the knowledge of the corporate IS group. When corporate IS is involved in developing an application, they participate in setting priorities, defining its essential features, and in software sourcing. Regardless of who develops an application, it is the user who ultimately decides to develop the application and what features to include.

TABLE 9.17   **CORP-F's IT Decision-Making Pattern**

Corporate IS	Divisional IS	Line Management
* Planning, development, and project management for non-user developed applications	None	* Initiates IS projects
* Operations		* Sets priorities for application development
* Advisory/consultant		* Specifies needs for non-user developed applications
		* Plans, develops, and manages user-developed applications

Applications, thus, are acquired in one of three ways: by line managers using a fourth generation language, by the corporate IS group, or from an outside vendor. The corporate IS group is always involved when applications are acquired through the latter two means. Users are charged only for software purchased from outside and are not charged for the services of the corporate IS group. Of course, applications developed by line units do bear the direct cost of the people involved in the application development effort.

CORP-F management views the IS function as somewhat more decentralized than other staff departments (most other staff activity is highly centralized). The corporate IS group has been much more inclined to limit its responsibility to establishing the environment, training line personnel, and acting as consultants.

Differences Across Divisions

Few differences exist in patterns of IT decision making across departments or subsidiaries. However, departments do differ with regard to the relative level of sophistication of their IT use. Some are aggressive users and major developers of fourth-generation language applications, while others have done little beyond automating their basic business functions. To a large extent, CORP-F has "passed the buck" in applying IT to the business unit.

Rationale

CORP-F has chosen its approach to IS decision making for four reasons:

1. They believed their small size and the homogeneous nature of their business offered very real economies through establishing common hardware and operations platforms across the business.

2. They viewed the "blue sky" committees as an effective way to educate managers on the potential applications offered by the interactive computing environment and to sell management on the value of IT.

3. Passing responsibility for proposing applications to the users was done to ensure that the applications were, in fact, wanted and that their features reflected user needs.

4. Use of a fourth-generation language for application development and the training of non-IS personnel in its use is seen as a means of minimizing the need for IS personnel.

Critical Success Factors

Table 9.18 lists those factors that CORP-F believed are necessary for them to be successful in applying IT. These factors fall into two principle categories:

1. Those reflecting the capabilities of the IS staff (Factors 1-4).

2.   Those representing the constraints of the organization's financial environment (Factors 5 and 6).

TABLE 9.18   **CORP-F's Critical Success Factors**

1. Strong IS senior executive with good interpersonal skills
2. Good strategic IT planning with participation by line managers
3. User confidence in competence of IS staff and integrity of implemented information systems
4. High system up-time and reliability
5. Economic pay-off to user in early stages of new application
6. Cost-effective applications and operations

Corporation G

Corporation G (CORP-G) is a relatively small (approximately $230 million in sales), young firm in the computer industry. Its growth has occurred solely through internal forces. While CORP-G has enjoyed considerable success, it is currently experiencing some sluggishness in its major markets.

As most of CORP-G's product line has evolved from a related technological base, it should not be surprising that the firm is functionally organized or that historically it has employed a centralized style of management. The company is now in transition from a purely centralized management style to one where divisional managers are being given some autonomy.

Information Services Background

The management of CORP-G's IS activities reflects an overall management philosophy toward centralization. While IT decision making has been very centralized, movement toward decentralization has occurred just in the past year as application development moved into the divisions. Divisional IS groups report directly to the division vice presidents.

As can be seen from Table 9.19, CORP-G seems to have benefited from its centralized approach to IT management. Two items in particular are noteworthy:

1.   It is applying IT well toward both business operations and strategies.

2.   It applies both current and sophisticated IT.

Despite these benefits, interviewees reported that considerable user dissatisfaction existed prior to the recent decentralization of application development. While the centralized IS staff had built a strong technological infrastructure and implemented numerous important information systems, it had little credibility with line management.

TABLE 9.19   **CORP-G's IT Environment**

Late adopter
Very good IT use in support of business operations
Good IT use in support of business strategies
Very sophisticated

Production data in DBMS:	80%
Interactive applications:	90%
Fourth-generation language applications:	0%
Micros linked via LANs:	100%
Number of mainframes/minis:	5
Number of micros:	200
Corporate IS head count:	35
Divisional IS head count:	45

Distribution of IT Decision Making

CORP-G's corporate IS group continues to serve a dominant role in managing IT. Table 9.20 shows that, aside from application development, little is handled outside the corporate IS group. Most development activities have been moved to the divisional IS groups, where applications are analyzed, designed, developed, and implemented. However, all information systems are designed and developed within architectural guidelines specified by the corporate IS group.

TABLE 9.20   **CORP-G's IT Decision-Making Pattern**

Corporate IS	Divisional IS	Line Management
* IT strategic planning	* Application development	* Initiates projects
* Provides the hardware/ software environment on which all applications run	* Manages small or primarily technical projects	* Sets priorities
* Determines the processes and technologies by which applications are developed		* Manages large or critical projects
* Operations		
* IT oversight		

The role served by line managers is interesting, since a majority of CORP-G's managers are knowledgable about and interested in IT (which is not unusual, given that CORP-G competes within the computer industry). Line managers do initiate most projects, set IT priorities, and actually manage key projects; and, the divisional vice-presidents make the final decision as to which applications are developed. However, there seemed to be a general attitude that line managers are not as involved in IT decisions as would be desired.

Differences Across Divisions

Few differences in IT decision responsibilities were found to exist.

Rationale

The main explanation given for decentralizing application development was not the planned dispersion of certain IT decision-making responsibilities but rather to improve the poor relationships that existed between users and the corporate IS group: users believed that the corporate IS group was neither sensitive to their needs nor provided adequate support to address user needs. By moving application development out to the divisions, it was hoped that line users would become more involved in development activities and that line managers would better understand the real costs and benefits associated with successful IT use. If the relations between users and the corporate IS group had not deteriorated, it is unlikely CORP-G would have decentralized application development.

There is general agreement that users have much better relations with the divisional IS groups than had existed with the corporate IS group. As a consequence, line managers are believed to have developed a better appreciation for the true potential and costs of IT use. For this reason, there is some expectation that further decentralization is likely to occur over the next three-to-five years.

Critical Success Factors

Table 9.21 lists those factors believed necessary by those interviewed for CORP-G to be successful in applying IT. These factors fall into three main categories:

1.   Those reflecting the capabilities of the IS staff (Factor 1).

2.   Those reflecting the capabilities of line management (Factors 2-4).

3.   Those representing the constraints of the organization's financial environment (Factors 5-6).

TABLE 9.21   **CORP-G's Critical Success Factors**

1. IS credibility
2. Line management understanding of IT and their IT needs
3. Realistic management expectations
4. Management commitment
5. Cost/benefit justification exists
6. Adequacy of IS budget

Given the history of information services at CORP-G, it is of interest that these factors are targeted mostly at line managers and not the IS staff or relations between the IS staff and line management. Such views seem supportive of the observation made earlier that moving application development to the divisions was primarily a strategy of improving IS/user relations and not an initial step in dispersing IT decision responsibilities to line managers.

Corporation H

Corporation H (CORP-H) is a small, closely held firm, in the mechanical and chemical bonding industry with approximately $200 million in sales. It has two principle areas of business and is organized into two corresponding business groups. One business group has two sub-units; the other has four. Sub-units are organized by products.

They characterize their business as a process industry. Their products are sold in containers for use by industrial customers. Most division management is housed in corporate headquarters or in close (three to four miles) proximity. Manufacturing plants are in remote locations.

Information Services Background

Information services has been a centralized activity at Corp E. All IS personnel report to a corporate IS executive and most are physically located at corporate headquarters. IT decision making is more centralized than other decision activities in the organization although this appears to be changing. One exception to this was data processing at manufacturing plants, which had been performed on distributed processors located in the plants. These processors, however, were removed within the past two years, with plants retaining processing capacity only for process control applications. Plant managements have supported the recentralization of data processing because they view a responsibility for hardware operations as interfering with their primary (i.e., manufacturing) responsibilities.

This movement toward increased processing centralization contrasts with a corresponding effort over the past two years to locate responsibility for initiating and developing applications closer to business units. Although all IS personnel report to a corporate IS manager, some have been physically moved to business units with all their efforts dedicated to a single business unit. This trend is expected to continue, with IS staff being located in business units as their volume of IS activity justifies full-time support. Business unit size, thus, is a primary limit to decentralization. It is unlikely that IS personnel will report to line managers in the near term, including those physically located in business units.

TABLE 9.22   **CORP-H's IT Environment**

Average with regard to adoption of IT
Very good IT use in support of business operations
Moderate to good IT use in support of business strategies
High sophistication

Production data in DBMS:	90%
Interactive applications:	90%
Fourth-generation language applications:	20%
Micros linked via LANs:	30%
Number of mainframes/minis:	9
Number of micros:	150
Corporate IS head count:	37
Divisional IS head count:	0

As indicated in Table 9.22, CORP-H has been and continues to be an active user of IT. Although they are average adopters of new IT, they have deployed technology more extensively than average once it has been adopted. Several other observations are noteworthy:

1. CORP-H has been quite successful in applying IT in support of both line operations and staff/administrative functions.

2. CORP-H has had only average success in developing and implementing strategic information systems. The success they have experienced appears to be in manufacturing applications.

3. The corporate and business unit IS head counts reflect the historical centralization of IT decision making but do not reflect the current physical assignment of IS staff in business units.

Distribution of IT Decision Making

CORP-H's corporate IS group plays the dominant role in managing IT. As can be seen in Table 9.23, corporate IS participates at all levels of the IT decision-making process. They make the decisions on vendors, computing capacities, and computer operations; and they participate with business units in long-range IT planning, application project prioritization and scope, and system implementation.

Line management proposes applications and application priorities for their areas of responsibility. This is a recent change precipitated by a switch in hardware vendor. Historically, priorities were set by a committee chaired by business unit IS staff. A new committee formed to set priorities for major new information systems is chaired by a divisional managers and comprised principally of line managers. This change reflects the increasing awareness by line management of IT's strategic importance.

TABLE 9.23   **CORP-H's IT Decision-Making Pattern**

Corporate IS	Divisional IS	Line Management
* IT planning	None	* Initiates projects
* Sets ling-term priorities		* Manages IT projects (when available)
* Provides personnel for application development		* Sets short-term IT priorities (subject to review by corporate IS)
* Operates all applications		* Proposes long-term priorities

When possible, the management of a development project is drawn from users with IS staff serving on the project team. Project committees are composed primarily of business unit personnel. They have responsibility for most implementation decisions subject to review by corporate IS.

Differences Across Divisions

There are few differences in the distribution of IT decision-making responsibilities across business units. Historical differences have been caused mostly by the physical distance between Corporate IS and operating units. For example, the use of distributed processors in manufacturing plants was attributed to the physical distances from corporate offices and limited telecommunications capabilities. New technology as well as a lessening of geographic boundaries separating line management and the corporate IS group are resulting in more uniform IT decision structures across business groups, units and functions.

Two primary trends are evident. First, corporate IS is assuming a more uniform responsibility for vendor, capacity, and operating decisions. Corporate IS decides these issues, handles application programming, and takes responsibility for computer operations. Second, the assignment of Corporate IS staff to business units is creating greater interest on the part of line management in IT and its use. This has directly resulted in line managers becoming more active in project initiation and management.

Rationale

Historically, CORP-H has justified the division of IT decision making on size and physical proximity. In earlier years, they were too small to realize the benefits of decentralizing IS staff because of the higher cost of doing so. Only those IS activities that could not be economically centralized because of physical distance from corporate headquarters were decentralized.

The recent movement toward a more decentralized structure for proposing and developing applications is occurring for the following reasons:

1. Some of their business groups and their respective product business units have grown large enough to support full-time IS staff. Other units will do so in the future.

2. It is held that the scope and priority of potential IT applications are better determined by line managers.

3. Quality of application development is much higher with active participation in the project by managers from the user group.

4. Successful strategic applications require heavy involvement by knowledgable business unit managers.

Critical Success Factors

Table 9.24 lists those factors that interviewees believed to be critical to CORP-H's successful application of IT. Three principle factors were identified:

1. Those characteristic of synergistic working relations between the IS staff and line management (Factors 1 and 2).

2. Those reflecting the capabilities of line management (Factors 3 and 4).

3. Those reflecting the capabilities of the IS staff (Factors 5 and 6).

TABLE 9.24 **CORP-H's Critical Success Factors**

1. Alignment of IT strategy with business strategy
2. Effective communications between line managers and IS staff
3. Line managers understand capabilities of IS personnel
4 Lline managers involvement in application proposals and development
5. IS staff understands the business
6. Proper definition of requirements

The perceived critical factors for success in applying IT are noteworthy given the historical centralization of IT decision making at CORP-H. In the two years IS staff members have been assigned full-time to specific business units, it has become widely perceived that a common, in-depth understanding between IS personnel and line managers is essential to successful IT use.

Appendix A
Research Methodology

The research consisted of two major phases: a field study and case studies. This overview of each phase is presented here to provide a richer context within which to understand and interpret the findings.

The Field Survey

The objective of the field survey was threefold:

1. To discover how firms have distributed IT management responsibilities among the corporate IS group, divisional IS groups, and non-IS (line) managers.

2. To identify organizational factors associated with particular patterns of IT management.

3 To assess the impact of these patterns on IT use and on organizational performance.

In our effort to reach these objectives, research design decisions were made regarding the unit of analysis, the data items to be collected, the respondents within each firm, the firms to be surveyed, and the data collection procedures.

Unit of Analysis

It was decided to focus on the *business unit* as the study's unit of analysis, that is, the base level at which data would be collected and analyzed. Depending on the structure of the organization involved, a business unit might be a functional division, a line of business, or a subsidiary company. Such a strategy was adopted for four major reasons:

1. IT use is linked with the nature and volume of information processing that occurs within a business unit.

2. IT use is linked to a business unit's senior management values regarding IT.

3. IT use is linked to the nature and amount of resources (financial and human) allocated to IS activities by a business unit.

4. IT use at any given point in time is linked with a business unit's history regarding IT.

Since these four factors tend to vary across an organization's business units, data analyzed at an organization-wide level are likely to "miss" these business unit distinctions; and, hence, an accurate understanding of the organizational phenomena being studied is less likely. Additionally, in order to increase the sensitivity of the research in detecting patterns between IT management strategy and business unit behaviors, attention was focused on three business units in each organization: a high-performing unit, an average performing unit, and a low-performing unit.

Data Items

The research team worked closely with the project's steering committee over a four-month period to identify the nature of the data items to be collected and to design an appropriate survey instrument. Although many data items were relevant to the project's objectives (data on the firm, on each business unit, on IT infrastructure, on the distribution of IT management responsibilities, on the quality of relations between IS personnel and users, and on IT use) it was acknowledged that respondents would most likely resist filling out a lengthy survey instrument. As a result, much debate ensued as to which data items had to be collected to achieve the study's objectives and how best to present the questions in order to ease the burden on respondents. A survey design expert at the Univeristy of North Carolina at Chapel Hill was also consulted. The results of this effort—the survey instruments—are provided as Appendices B through D.

Respondents

Another important facet of this research design was the decision to have multiple respondents from each organization. Three main reasons prompted such a strategy:

1. No single individual could be expected to have a working understanding of all the issues being examined. Ideally, data gathered on each issue should reflect the views of an individual intimately familiar with the issue.

2. Different individuals might very well hold different views on many of these issues (e.g., quality of information services, business unit performance, distribution of IT management responsibilities, etc.). By having several individuals provide their views on such issues, it is possible to compare responses as a means of coping with the biases of a particular individual.

3. The effort required by each respondent is reduced.

Accordingly, five individuals in each firm completed a research instrument: the firm's chief financial officer (CFO) (the three-page instrument shown as Appendix B), the firm's senior IS executive (CIO) officer (the four-page instrument shown as Appendix C), and the senior executive of each of three selected business units (the six-page instrument shown as Appendix D). Table A.1 summarizes the research issues directed toward each of these individuals.

TABLE A.1   **Survey Item Summary by Respondent**

Respondent	*Topics*
Chief financial officer	—Corporate business environment —Corporate centralization —Corporate strategic posture —Corporate performance —Operating unit performance
Chief information officer	—Quality of services provided each operating unit —Relations between corporate IS function and operating units —Corporate IT infrastructure —Structure of corporate IS function —Distribution of IT management responsibilities
Business unit general manager	—Quality of services provided by corporate and divisional IS groups —Relations with corporate and divisional IS groups —Operating unit business environment —Operating unit strategic posture —Operating unit performance —Operating unit IT use —Distribution of IT management responsibilities

Firms Sampled

The focus of this study was *not* to examine "leading edge" (regarding IT use) firms but rather to examine a random sample of business organizations. This decision was made for two main reasons:

1. Such a sample might be more meaningfully used as a 'benchmark' by interested executives.

2. Observed patterns of IT management responsibilities would more accurately reflect 'deep' trends occurring across business organizations.

Any random sample of firms, however, might be expected to include some who might be considered "leading edge."

To carry out this design, a sampling of the Financial Executives Institute (FEI) membership produced a group of 140 firms that indicated a willingness to participate in this research project. All 140 firms were sent the research instruments. The study's final data base included completed instruments from 78 business units representing 35 organizations (a 25 percent response rate).

While this response rate is low, it is not unexpected given the nature of this research design (*lengthy* questionnaires distributed to *many* senior managers within sampled organizations) and not too dissimilar from survey sample research in general. Follow-up letters to firms not responding produced very similar explanations as to why participation was declined:

— Current business commitments prohibit participation at this time.

— Corporate merger/acquisition activities prohibit participation at this time.

— Reorganization of the firm's IS activities prohibit participation at this time.

— Major changes in the IT infrastructure prohibit participation at this time.

The main concern with low survey response rates involves the randomness of the sample of participating firms. Given the wide range in responses with most of the data items, we are satisfied that this sample of organizations does not represent any particular set of biases.

Data Collection Procedures

A short description of the research project was included in a mailing to FEI chapters in May 1987, along with a request that the description be read at the next chapter meeting in order to inform members that their firms might be selected as participants and to encourage participation. Subsequently, a package containing the five survey instruments (Appendix B, Appendix C, and three copies of Appendix D) was mailed in June 1987 to the CFO of the 140 firms that had initially agreed to participate.

Instructions attached to the CFO survey instrument (see Appendix B) explained the aims and benefits of the project, provided assurance that a firm's responses would be kept confidential, and requested that the CFO:

1. Answer and return the CFO instrument.

2. Identify high-, average-, and low-performing business units.

3. Note these three business units on the CIO survey (Appendix C).

4. Direct appropriate survey instruments to the CIO and the three senior business unit executives and request that these individuals complete the instrument and return it to the research team. As can be seen in

Appendices C and D, these instruments also contained an overview that described the aims and benefits of the research project.

The follow-up letter to nonrespondents was mailed in late August 1987, and the data collection phase of the field survey was ended in September 1987.

Case Studies

The objective of the case studies was twofold:

1. To confirm the findings of the field survey. In other words, did the responses to the field survey instruments reflect the situations observed at the case study sites?

2. To better understand the forces that lay behind the distribution of IT management responsibilities at each case study site.

In our effort to reach these objectives, research design decisions again were made regarding the unit of analysis, the information to be gathered, the respondents within each firm, the firms to be studied, and the information gathering procedures.

Unit of Analysis

For the same reasons as given for the field survey, the unit of analysis was the *business unit*. Specifically, the business units in which interviews were held are those selected by the CFO in the field survey.

Information

The questions given in Table A.2 were used as a means of introducing the issues to be examined. The conversations that ensued covered a much broader range of topics.

Respondents

A major objective of these case studies was to acquire a rich understanding of the IT environment and IT management history of each case study organization. As a result, four individuals were interviewed: the CIO, and the senior IS manager within each of the three business units examined in the field survey. We believed that these individuals are precisely those who would be most familiar with the key events and the reasoning that lay behind each firm's past and current IT management strategies.

TABLE A.2   **Case Study Questions**

1. Describe the distribution of IT management responsibilities between corporate IS and divisional IS groups in applying IT. Why?

2. How does such a distribution compare with overall corporate centralization/decentralization policies?

3. Describe the distribution of IT management responsibilities between divisional IS personnel and line managers in applying IT. Why?

4. Have these patterns of responsibilities changed over the last 3-5 years? If so, how and why?

5. Do these patterns of responsibilities differ across business units? If so, how do they differ and why do they differ?

6. What are the critical factors that need to be in place for business units to apply IT effectively? Why?

7. What are the factors that most limit a business unit's capability to apply IT effectively? Why?

8. Are these factors (both positive and negative) influenced by the distribution of IT management responsibilities?

9. Why might a firm exhibit a pattern of IT management responsibilities opposite to that observed in your firm and still apply IT effectively?

Firms Studied

Based on the results of the field survey, eight firms were studied:

— Two that exhibited an *average* pattern of IT decision making based on our analysis of survey data. That is, the involvement of corporate IS, business unit IS, and line management was similar to "average" responses obtained in the field survey.

— Two that exhibited a *shared* pattern of IT decision making. That is, corporate IS, divisional IS, and line management "shared" involvement in many, if not most, IT management responsibilities.

— Two that exhibited a *centralized* pattern of IT decision making. That is, corporate IS was primarily responsible for IT management.

— Two that exhibited a *decentralized* pattern of IT decision making. That is, managers in the business units were primarily responsible for IT management.

In selecting a particular firm to represent one of the above four patterns of IT management responsibility, the criteria used sought to include: small, medium and large firms; and, firms experiencing favorable business performance, IT use, and IS/line manager relations in at least one, and ideally more than one, business unit but which exhibited some variation in these measures across business units.

Information Gathering Procedures

The CFOs of the eight firms were each contacted by phone in February 1988 and asked if their firms would be willing to serve as a case study site. An affirmative answer was received from each individual contacted. Each CFO was then asked for the names and phone numbers of the four individuals mentioned earlier: the CIO and the senior IS manager in each of the three business units. Each of these individuals was then contacted in March 1988 by phone and asked if they would be willing to be interviewed. In each case, an affirmative answer was received. The actual interview either took place at this time, or was scheduled at a later, mutually agreeable time. On average, each of these interviews lasted just under one hour in length.

Appendix B
CFO Questionnaire

Please indicate your answer to questions 1 and 2 by circling the appropriate response using the following format:

no extent   some extent   moderate extent   great extent   very great extent

1. When *senior management* meets, to what extent do discussions focus on each of the following:

   a. suppliers   no some mod great very great
   b. competitors   no some mod great very great
   c. customers   no some mod great very great
   d. investors   no some mod great very great
   e. labor   no some mod great very great
   f. regulatory agencies   no some mod great very great

2. Over the past *two years,* to what extent have each of the following *changed?* (For example, entry of new competitors, fewer sources of supply, new federal regulations, etc.)

   a. suppliers   no some mod great very great
   b. competitors   no some mod great very great
   c. customers   no some mod great very great
   d. investors   no some mod great very great
   e. labor   no some mod great very great
   f. regulatory agencies   no some mod great very great

Please use the following response format provided to answer question 3.

does not make decision	minor role in decision	shares equally in decision
1	2	3

primary role in decision	unilaterally makes decision
4	5

3. To what extent are *important decisions shared* by corporate and business unit management for each of the following business activities? Please circle the appropriate number for *each* level of management.

	Corporate Management					*Business Unit Management*				
a. inbound/outbound logistics	1	2	3	4	5	1	2	3	4	5
b. manufacturing	1	2	3	4	5	1	2	3	4	5
c. marketing	1	2	3	4	5	1	2	3	4	5
d. sales	1	2	3	4	5	1	2	3	4	5
e. customer service	1	2	3	4	5	1	2	3	4	5
f. personnel/human resources	1	2	3	4	5	1	2	3	4	5
g. engineering/R&D	1	2	3	4	5	1	2	3	4	5
h. finance/accounting	1	2	3	4	5	1	2	3	4	5
i. treasury	1	2	3	4	5	1	2	3	4	5

Please read the four descriptions of potential enterprise strategies that follow before answering question 4.

analyzer   analyzes industry changes but tends to ignore those having no direct influence on current areas of operations
maintains a secure market niche with relatively stable product lines
offers a limited range of products or services

prospector   values being first in new product and market areas
operates within broad, periodically changing product lines
may not choose to maintain strength in all market areas it enters

reactor   reacts quickly to follow a limited set of promising new industry developments
maintains a stable, limited line of products
is seldom first in with new products

defender   defending existing product lines is a primary objective
aggressive only when risk is low or action is forced by outside pressures

4. Circle the *description* that best fits your enterprise for *each* of the time periods indicated.

   a. 3–5 years ago   analyzer   prospector   reactor   defender
   b. today   analyzer   prospector   reactor   defender
   c. 3–5 years from now   analyzer   prospector   reactor   defender

5. Enter your enterprise's average (after-tax) *return on total assets* for each of the past three years.

   1986: _____ %   1985: _____ %   1984: _____ %

6. Indicate your enterprise's *annual sales growth* for each of the past three years.

   1986: _____ %   1985: _____ %   1984: _____ %

7. Circle the percentage of *ideal or optimum* performance you believe your enterprise has achieved over the past three years.

   10   20   30   40   50   60   70   80   90   100

8. Circle the percentage of firms in your industry that your enterprise has *outperformed* over the past three years.

   10   20   30   40   50   60   70   80   90   100

Please answer question 9 by circling the appropriate letter for each item, using the following response format:

Excellent	Good	Average	Fair	Poor
A	B	C	D	E

9. The three business units were identified as A, B, and C in the *overview* of the project on page 1 of this questionnaire. Please rate the *average performance* of each *business unit* over the last three years on each of the items listed.

	Business Unit A	Business Unit B	Business Unit C
Financial Performance			
sales growth	A B C D E not applicable	A B C D E not applicable	A B C D E not applicable
market share	A B C D E not applicable	A B C D E not applicable	A B C D E not applicable
sales revenue	A B C D E not applicable	A B C D E not applicable	A B C D E not applicable
operating profits	A B C D E not applicable	A B C D E not applicable	A B C D E not applicable
cash flow from operations	A B C D E not applicable	A B C D E not applicable	A B C D E not applicable
return on investment	A B C D E not applicable	A B C D E not applicable	A B C D E not applicable
Market Performance			
market development	A B C D E not applicable	A B C D E not applicable	A B C D E not applicable
product development	A B C D E not applicable	A B C D E not applicable	A B C D E not applicable
product quality	A B C D E not applicable	A B C D E not applicable	A B C D E not applicable
service quality	A B C D E not applicable	A B C D E not applicable	A B C D E not applicable

Manufacturing Performance

	Unit 1	Unit 2	Unit 3
process improvement	A B C D E not applicable	A B C D E not applicable	A B C D E not applicable
productivity	A B C D E not applicable	A B C D E not applicable	A B C D E not applicable
cost control	A B C D E not applicable	A B C D E not applicable	A B C D E not applicable

Others

personnel development	A B C D E not applicable	A B C D E not applicable	A B C D E not applicable
political/public affairs	A B C D E not applicable	A B C D E not applicable	A B C D E not applicable

Please answer question 10 by circling the appropriate number for each item using the following response format:

not important	somewhat important	important	very important	extremely important
1	2	3	4	5

10. Rate the *importance* of each performance measure for evaluating *each business unit.*

	Business Unit A	Business Unit B	Business Unit C
Financial Performance			
sales growth	1 2 3 4 5	1 2 3 4 5	1 2 3 4 5
market share	1 2 3 4 5	1 2 3 4 5	1 2 3 4 5
sales revenue	1 2 3 4 5	1 2 3 4 5	1 2 3 4 5
operating profits	1 2 3 4 5	1 2 3 4 5	1 2 3 4 5
profit to sales ratio	1 2 3 4 5	1 2 3 4 5	1 2 3 4 5
cash flow from operations	1 2 3 4 5	1 2 3 4 5	1 2 3 4 5
return on investment	1 2 3 4 5	1 2 3 4 5	1 2 3 4 5
Market Performance			
market development	1 2 3 4 5	1 2 3 4 5	1 2 3 4 5
product development	1 2 3 4 5	1 2 3 4 5	1 2 3 4 5
product quality	1 2 3 4 5	1 2 3 4 5	1 2 3 4 5
service quality	1 2 3 4 5	1 2 3 4 5	1 2 3 4 5
Manufacturing Performance			
process improvement	1 2 3 4 5	1 2 3 4 5	1 2 3 4 5
productivity	1 2 3 4 5	1 2 3 4 5	1 2 3 4 5
cost control	1 2 3 4 5	1 2 3 4 5	1 2 3 4 5
Others			
personnel development	1 2 3 4 5	1 2 3 4 5	1 2 3 4 5
political/public affairs	1 2 3 4 5	1 2 3 4 5	1 2 3 4 5

Thank you for your cooperation in completing this questionnaire. Your willingness to participate will help ensure the success of our project. Your firm will receive a summary of the study's results.

Appendix C
CIO Questionnaire

The first six questions refer to a number of issues about your delivery of IS services to each of the three business units identified as *A, B, and C in the overview of the project on the first page of this questionnaire.*

1. Please fill in the appropriate percentage of your current total IS services provided to each of the business units. (Note: Percentages will not sum to 100% unless these three business units represent your entire user base.)

        Unit A: _____ %   Unit B: _____ %   Unit C: _____ %

For questions 2–6, please circle the appropriate response for each business unit, using the following format:

no extent   **some extent**   **moderate extent**   **great extent**   **very great extent**

	Business Unit A	*Business Unit B*	*Business Unit C*
2. To what extent are the corporate IS services provided to each business unit:			
a. reliable?	no some mod great very great	no some mod great very great	no some mod great very great
b. of high quality?	no some mod great very great	no some mod great very great	no some mod great very great
c. timely?	no some mod great very great	no some mod great very great	no some mod great very great

3. To what extent are *commitments made by business units* to corporate IS carried out?

      no some mod great very great   no some mod great very great   no some mod great very great

4. To what extent is your corporate IS function actively involved in:

a. proposing new business unit IS services?	no some mod great very great	no some mod great very great	no some mod great very great
b. acquiring business unit IS services?	no some mod great very great	no some mod great very great	no some mod great very great
c. planning for future business unit IS services?	no some mod great very great	no some mod great very great	no some mod great very great

5. To what extent do your corporate IS function and each business unit:

a. agree on needs, opportunities and problems?	no some mod great very great	no some mod great very great	no some mod great very great
b. have the same goals and objectives?	no some mod great very great	no some mod great very great	no some mod great very great
c. share the same priorities?	no some mod great very great	no some mod great very great	no some mod great very great
d. resolve conflict without referring to higher authority?	no some mod great very great	no some mod great very great	no some mod great very great

6. To what extent do your *corporate IS* personnel understand each business unit's:

	Business Unit A	Business Unit B	Business Unit C
a. operations?	no some mod great very great	no some mod great very great	no some mod great very great
b. strategies?	no some mod great very great	no some mod great very great	no some mod great very great
c. management practices?	no some mod great very great	no some mod great very great	no some mod great very great

7. Please circle the year that your enterprise first installed each of the following technologies:

a. microcomputer   pre-'78 '78 '79 '80 '81 '82 '83 '84 '85 '86 not yet
b. data base management system   pre-'78 '78 '79 '80 '81 '82 '83 '84 '85 '86 not yet
c. external data service   pre-'78 '78 '79 '80 '81 '82 '83 '84 '85 '86 not yet
d. information center   pre-'78 '78 '79 '80 '81 '82 '83 '84 '85 '86 not yet
e. data base administrator   pre-'78 '78 '79 '80 '81 '82 '83 '84 '85 '86 not yet
f. local area network   pre-'78 '78 '79 '80 '81 '82 '83 '84 '85 '86 not yet
g. electronic mail   pre-'78 '78 '79 '80 '81 '82 '83 '84 '85 '86 not yet

Questions 8 and 9 refer to your existing IS resource base.

8. Please fill in the *approximate number* for each of the following items:

a. headcount of the corporate IS group   _____
b. headcount of all IS staff in the enterprise   _____
c. number of mainframe and minicomputers in the enterprise   _____
d. number of microcomputers in the enterprise   _____
e. number of installed LANs   _____
f. number of managerial/professional employees   _____
g. number of managerial/professional employees with work stations _____
h. number of enterprise senior executives   _____
i. number of enterprise senior executives with work stations   _____

9. Please circle the *approximate percentage* for each of the following items:

a. enterprise production data maintained within a
data base management system   0   10   20   30   40   50   60   70   80   90   100
b. mainstream business applications
that are interactive   0   10   20   30   40   50   60   70   80   90   100
c. applications developed by your IS staff
using a fourth-generation language   0   10   20   30   40   50   60   70   80   90   100
d. microcomputers linked by LANs   0   10   20   30   40   50   60   70   80   90   100

Question 10-13 refer to the organization of IS services delivery in your enterprise.

10. Please list the *titles* of all individuals, if any, between the chief executive and yourself in the management heirarchy.

CEO _____ _____ _____ _____ yourself

11. Are you a member of your enterprise's executive committee?

_____ yes   _____ no

12. Which of the following best describes to whom *business unit IS managers* report; please circle the appropriate letter.

a. report to corporate IS manager
b. report to business unit manager
c. report to corporate IS manager with dotted-line responsibility to business unit manager
d. report to business unit manager with dotted-line responsibility to corporate IS manager
e. other (please specify) _____

13. Which of the following best describes the organization of your corporate IS function; please circle the appropriate letter.

   a. an independent subsidiary?

   b. profit center?

   c. service center with costs allocated to business units receiving IS services?

   d. service center with costs not allocated to business units receiving IS services?

   e. other (please specify) _____

Questions 14–18 ask you to indicate who has decision responsibility for a variety of IS decisions. For each question, indicate the level of involvement of each of four management groups, by circling the appropriate number *for each management group in each question,* **using the following response format:**

does not make decision	minor role in decision	shares equally in decision
1	2	3
primary role in decision	**unilaterally makes decision**	**do not know**
4	5	?

14. Please indicate who makes (or shares) the following *hardware decisions* for *business unit long-range (3–5 years) IS services plan* for each business unit:

	Corporate		Business Unit		Do Not Know
	corporate IS management	other corporate management	business unit IS management	other business unit management	
a. specific vendors, brands, or technologies?					
i. mainframes/minicomputers	1 2 3 4 5	1 2 3 4 5	1 2 3 4 5	1 2 3 4 5	?
ii. microcomputers	1 2 3 4 5	1 2 3 4 5	1 2 3 4 5	1 2 3 4 5	?
iii. telecommunications	1 2 3 4 5	1 2 3 4 5	1 2 3 4 5	1 2 3 4 5	?
b. capacity to be acquired for:					
i. mainframes/minicomputers	1 2 3 4 5	1 2 3 4 5	1 2 3 4 5	1 2 3 4 5	?
ii. microcomputers	1 2 3 4 5	1 2 3 4 5	1 2 3 4 5	1 2 3 4 5	?
iii. telecommunications	1 2 3 4 5	1 2 3 4 5	1 2 3 4 5	1 2 3 4 5	?

15. Indicate who is responsible (or shares responsibility) for *selecting* the *IS applications* to be included in the long-range (3–5 years) *business unit plans* in each of the following areas:

	Corporate		Business Unit		Do Not Know
	corporate IS management	other corporate management	business unit IS management	other business unit management	
i. inbound/outbound logistics	1 2 3 4 5	1 2 3 4 5	1 2 3 4 5	1 2 3 4 5	?
ii. manufacturing	1 2 3 4 5	1 2 3 4 5	1 2 3 4 5	1 2 3 4 5	?
iii. marketing	1 2 3 4 5	1 2 3 4 5	1 2 3 4 5	1 2 3 4 5	?
iv. sales/customer service	1 2 3 4 5	1 2 3 4 5	1 2 3 4 5	1 2 3 4 5	?
v. engineering/R&D	1 2 3 4 5	1 2 3 4 5	1 2 3 4 5	1 2 3 4 5	?
vi. finance/accounting	1 2 3 4 5	1 2 3 4 5	1 2 3 4 5	1 2 3 4 5	?

16. Please indicate who has (or shares) decision responsibility for the following elements of each business unit's *annual IS services plan:*

	Corporate		Business Unit		Do Not Know
	corporate IS management	other corporate management	business unit IS management	other business unit management	
a. capacities to be acquired					
i. mainframes/microcomputers	1 2 3 4 5	1 2 3 4 5	1 2 3 4 5	1 2 3 4 5	?
ii. microcomputers	1 2 3 4 5	1 2 3 4 5	1 2 3 4 5	1 2 3 4 5	?
iii. telecommunications	1 2 3 4 5	1 2 3 4 5	1 2 3 4 5	1 2 3 4 5	?
b. extensive IS service additions or enhancements for					
i. inbound/outbound logistics	1 2 3 4 5	1 2 3 4 5	1 2 3 4 5	1 2 3 4 5	?
ii. manufacturing	1 2 3 4 5	1 2 3 4 5	1 2 3 4 5	1 2 3 4 5	?
iii. marketing	1 2 3 4 5	1 2 3 4 5	1 2 3 4 5	1 2 3 4 5	?
iv. sales/customer service	1 2 3 4 5	1 2 3 4 5	1 2 3 4 5	1 2 3 4 5	?
v. engineering/R&D	1 2 3 4 5	1 2 3 4 5	1 2 3 4 5	1 2 3 4 5	?
vi. finance/accounting	1 2 3 4 5	1 2 3 4 5	1 2 3 4 5	1 2 3 4 5	?

Please circle the appropriate number *for each management group in each question,* using the following response format:

does not make decision	minor role in decision	shares equally in decision
1	2	3

primary role in decision	unilaterally makes decision	do not know
4	5	?

17. Indicate who has (or shares) decision responsibility for the following elements of *current business unit IS* projects:

	Corporate		Business Unit		Do Not Know
	corporate IS management	other corporate management	business unit IS management	other business unit management	
a. project management	1 2 3 4 5	1 2 3 4 5	1 2 3 4 5	1 2 3 4 5	?
b. essential features and functions to be provided	1 2 3 4 5	1 2 3 4 5	1 2 3 4 5	1 2 3 4 5	?

18. Indicate who has (or shares) decision responsibility for *day-to-day IS operations* that support each business unit:

	Corporate		Business Unit		Do Not Know
	corporate IS management	other corporate management	business unit IS management	other business unit management	
a. setting service delivery priorities when unforeseen problems arise	1 2 3 4 5	1 2 3 4 5	1 2 3 4 5	1 2 3 4 5	?
b. overriding standard procedures when special IS service needs arise	1 2 3 4 5	1 2 3 4 5	1 2 3 4 5	1 2 3 4 5	?
c. evaluating the quality of IS services	1 2 3 4 5	1 2 3 4 5	1 2 3 4 5	1 2 3 4 5	?

Thank you for your cooperation in completing this questionnaire. Your willingness to participate will help ensure the success of our project. Your firm will receive a summary of the study's results.

Appendix D
Business Unit Manager Questionnaire

Two primary sources of IS services are the corporate IS group and your business unit's own IS group. The first six questions refer to these services and those who provide them. Please begin by answering the following question:

1. Over the past *year*, approximately what percentage of total IS services were provided to your business unit by corporate IS and by business unit IS? (Note: It is possible that the two percentages will not sum to 100%.)

   ____ % corporate IS   (the primary provider of IS services within your enterprise other than those provided within your business unit)

   ____ % business unit IS   (IS services provided within your business unit)

Please answer questions 2–6 by circling the appropriate response for each of the two IS groups just identified, using the following response format:

no extent	some extent	moderate extent	great extent	very great extent

	Corporate IS	*Business Unit IS*
2. To what extent are the IS services received from each IS group:		
a. reliable?	no some mod great very great	no some mod great very great
b. of high quality?	no some mod great very great	no some mod great very great
c. timely?	no some mod great very great	no some mod great very great
3. To what extent are commitments made by each IS group carried out?	no some mod great very great	no some mod great very great
4. To what extent is each IS group actively involved in each of the following for your business unit?		
a. proposing new IS services?	no some mod great very great	no some mod great very great
b. acquiring IS services?	no some mod great very great	no some mod great very great
c. planning for future IS services?	no some mod great very great	no some mod great very great
5. To what extent does your business unit and each IS group:		
a. agree on needs, opportunities, and problems?	no some mod great very great	no some mod great very great
b. have the same goals and objectives?	no some mod great very great	no some mod great very great
c. share the same priorities?	no some mod great very great	no some mod great very great
d. resolve conflict without referring to higher authority?	no some mod great very great	no some mod great very great
6. To what extent do personnel from each IS group understand your unit's:		
a. operations?	no some mod great very great	no some mod great very great
b. strategies?	no some mod great very great	no some mod great very great
c. management practices?	no some mod great very great	no some mod great very great

Please answer questions 7–10 by circling the appropriate response using the following format:

no extent   **some extent**   **moderate extent**   **great extent**   **very great extent**

7. To what extent do your *operating managers* view IS services as:
   a. an integral part of unit operations?   no   some   mod   great   very great
   b. an integral part of unit strategy?   no   some   mod   great   very great
   c. a means of improving their personal performance?   no   some   mod   great   very great

8. To what extent are your *operating managers* actively involved in each of the following for your unit:
   a. proposing new IS services?   no   some   mod   great   very great
   b. acquiring IS services?   no   some   mod   great   very great
   c. planning for future IS services?   no   some   mod   great   very great

9. When your managers meet, to what extent do discussions focus on each of the following:
   a. suppliers?   no   some   mod   great   very great
   b. competitors?   no   some   mod   great   very great
   c. customers?   no   some   mod   great   very great
   d. labor?   no   some   mod   great   very great
   e. regulatory agencies?   no   some   mod   great   very great

10. Over the past *two years*, to what extent have each of the following *changed* (for example, entry of new competitors, fewer sources of supply, new federal regulations, etc.):
    a. suppliers?   no   some   mod   great   very great
    b. competitors?   no   some   mod   great   very great
    c. customers?   no   some   mod   great   very great
    d. labor?   no   some   mod   great   very great
    e. regulatory agencies?   no   some   mod   great   very great

The following question uses a different response format than the preceeding.

11. How accurately do the following statements describe competition in your industry?
    a. When one firm reduces prices, all firms
       react quickly with similar reductions.   very accurate   1   2   3   4   5   not at all accurate
    b. When one firm introduces a sales promotion
       campaign, all firms react with their own campaigns.   very accurate   1   2   3   4   5   not at all accurate
    c. When one firm introduces new manufacturing tech-
       nology, all firms introduce similar technologies.   very accurate   1   2   3   4   5   not at all accurate
    d. All firms react quickly to any loss of
       market share.   very accurate   1   2   3   4   5   not at all accurate

Please read the four descriptions of potential business unit strategies that follow before answering question 12.

analyzer   analyzes industry changes but tends to ignore those having no direct influence on current areas of operations
maintains a secure market niche with relatively stable product lines
offers a limited range of products or services

prospector   values being first in new product and market areas
operates within broad, periodically changing product lines
may not choose to maintain strength in all market areas it enters

reactor   reacts quickly to follow a limited set of promising new industry developments
maintains a stable, limited line of products
is seldom first in with new products

defender   defending existing product lines is a primary objective
aggressive only when risk is low or action is forced by outside pressures

12. Circle the description that best fits your business unit for *each* of the time periods indicated.

a. 3–5 years ago	analyzer	prospector	reactor	defender
b. today	analyzer	prospector	reactor	defender
c. 3–5 years from now	analyzer	prospector	reactor	defender

13. Rate the *average performance* of your business unit in meeting your goals and objectives in each of the areas listed over the last three years. Answer question 13 by circling the appropriate letter for each item using the following response format.

excellent	good	average	fair	poor
A	B	C	D	E

Financial Performance

a. sales growth   A B C D E not applicable
b. market share   A B C D E not applicable
c. sales volume   A B C D E not applicable
d. operating profits   A B C D E not applicable
e. profit-to-sales ratio   A B C D E not applicable
f. cash flow from operations   A B C D E not applicable
g. return on investment   A B C D E not applicable

Product Performance

h. market development   A B C D E not applicable
i. product development   A B C D E not applicable
j. product quality   A B C D E not applicable
k. service quality   A B C D E not applicable

Manufacturing Performance

l. process improvement   A B C D E not applicable
m. productivity   A B C D E not applicable
n. cost control   A B C D E not applicable

Others

o. personnel development   A B C D E not applicable
p. political/public affairs   A B C D E not applicable

14. Please identify the four performance measures in question 13 that are most important to you in assessing the performance of your business unit by circling the letter in front of each of these four measures.

Please answer questions 15–20 by circling the appropriate response, using the following format:

no extent	some extent	moderate extent	great extent	very great extent

	15. To what extent is each of the following activities *important* to the success of your business unit:	**16.** To what extent is your business unit *successful* in carrying out each of the following activities:	**17.** To what extent does your business unit *rely on IS services* for accomplishing each of the following activities:
Line Operations			
a. inbound/outbound logistics?	no some mod great very great	no some mod great very great	no some mod great very great
b. manufacturing?	no some mod great very great	no some mod great very great	no some mod great very great
c. marketing?	no some mod great very great	no some mod great very great	no some mod great very great
d. sales?	no some mod great very great	no some mod great very great	no some mod great very great
e. customer service?	no some mod great very great	no some mod great very great	no some mod great very great
Staff/Administrative Support			
f. personnel/human resources?	no some mod great very great	no some mod great very great	no some mod great very great
g. engineering/R&D?	no some mod great very great	no some mod great very great	no some mod great very great
h. planning?	no some mod great very great	no some mod great very great	no some mod great very great
i. finance/accounting?	no some mod great very great	no some mod great very great	no some mod great very great
j. treasury?	no some mod great very great	no some mod great very great	no some mod great very great

The next three questions focus on strategies for gaining competitive advantage. Please circle the appropriate response for each item, using the preceeding response format.

	18. To what extent is each of these strategies *important* to the success of your business unit?	**19.** To what extent is your business unit *successful* in carrying out each of these strategies?	**20.** To what extent does your business unit *rely on IS services* for accomplishing each of these strategies?
a. being low-cost producer	no some mod great very great	no some mod great very great	no some mod great very great
b. having manufacturing flexibility	no some mod great very great	no some mod great very great	no some mod great very great
c. enhancing supplier linkages	no some mod great very great	no some mod great very great	no some mod great very great
d. enhancing customer linkages	no some mod great very great	no some mod great very great	no some mod great very great
e. providing value-added services	no some mod great very great	no some mod great very great	no some mod great very great
f. enhancing existing products	no some mod great very great	no some mod great very great	no some mod great very great
g. introducing new products	no some mod great very great	no some mod great very great	no some mod great very great
h. entering new markets	no some mod great very great	no some mod great very great	no some mod great very great

In questions 21–25, please circle the appropriate number for each management group in each question, using the following response format:

does not make decision	minor role in decision	shares equally in decision
1	2	3

primary role in decision	unilaterally makes decision	do not know
4	5	?

21. Indicate who makes (or shares) the following *hardware decisions* for the *long-range (3-5 years) IS services plan* for your business unit:

	Corporate		Business Unit		Do Not Know
	corporate IS management	other corporate management	business unit IS management	other business unit management	
a. specific vendors, brands or technologies					
i. mainframes/minicomputers	1 2 3 4 5	1 2 3 4 5	1 2 3 4 5	1 2 3 4 5	?
ii. microcomputers	1 2 3 4 5	1 2 3 4 5	1 2 3 4 5	1 2 3 4 5	?
iii. telecommunications	1 2 3 4 5	1 2 3 4 5	1 2 3 4 5	1 2 3 4 5	?
b. capacities to be acquired for					
i. mainframes/minicomputers	1 2 3 4 5	1 2 3 4 5	1 2 3 4 5	1 2 3 4 5	?
ii. microcomputers	1 2 3 4 5	1 2 3 4 5	1 2 3 4 5	1 2 3 4 5	?
iii. telecommunications	1 2 3 4 5	1 2 3 4 5	1 2 3 4 5	1 2 3 4 5	?

22. Indicate who is responsible (or shares responsibility) for *selecting the IS applications to be included in your long-range (3—5 years) business unit IS service plan* in each of the following areas:

	Corporate		Business Unit		Do Not Know
	corporate IS management	other corporate management	business unit IS management	other business unit management	
a. inbound/outbound logistics	1 2 3 4 5	1 2 3 4 5	1 2 3 4 5	1 2 3 4 5	?
b. manufacturing	1 2 3 4 5	1 2 3 4 5	1 2 3 4 5	1 2 3 4 5	?
c. marketing	1 2 3 4 5	1 2 3 4 5	1 2 3 4 5	1 2 3 4 5	?
d. sales/customer service	1 2 3 4 5	1 2 3 4 5	1 2 3 4 5	1 2 3 4 5	?
e. engineering/R&D	1 2 3 4 5	1 2 3 4 5	1 2 3 4 5	1 2 3 4 5	?
f. finance/accounting	1 2 3 4 5	1 2 3 4 5	1 2 3 4 5	1 2 3 4 5	?

23. Indicate who has (or shares) decision responsibility for the following elements of your business unit's *annual IS services plan:*

	Corporate		Business Unit		Do Not Know
	corporate IS management	other corporate management	business unit IS management	other business unit management	
a. capacities to be acquired					
i. mainframes/minicomputers	1 2 3 4 5	1 2 3 4 5	1 2 3 4 5	1 2 3 4 5	?
ii. microcomputers	1 2 3 4 5	1 2 3 4 5	1 2 3 4 5	1 2 3 4 5	?
iii. telecommunications	1 2 3 4 5	1 2 3 4 5	1 2 3 4 5	1 2 3 4 5	?
b. extensive IS service additions or enhancements for					
i. inbound/outbound logistics	1 2 3 4 5	1 2 3 4 5	1 2 3 4 5	1 2 3 4 5	?
ii. manufacturing	1 2 3 4 5	1 2 3 4 5	1 2 3 4 5	1 2 3 4 5	?
iii. marketing	1 2 3 4 5	1 2 3 4 5	1 2 3 4 5	1 2 3 4 5	?
iv. sales/customer service	1 2 3 4 5	1 2 3 4 5	1 2 3 4 5	1 2 3 4 5	?
v. engineering/R&D	1 2 3 4 5	1 2 3 4 5	1 2 3 4 5	1 2 3 4 5	?
vi. finance/accounting	1 2 3 4 5	1 2 3 4 5	1 2 3 4 5	1 2 3 4 5	?

Please circle the appropriate number for *each management group in each question,* using the following response format:

does not make decision	minor role in decision	shares equally in decision
1	2	3

primary role in decision	unilaterally makes decision	do not know
4	5	?

24. Please indicate who has (or shares) decision responsibility for the following elements of your *current business unit IS projects:*

	Corporate		Business Unit		Do Not Know
	corporate IS management	other corporate management	business unit IS management	other business unit management	
a. project management	1 2 3 4 5	1 2 3 4 5	1 2 3 4 5	1 2 3 4 5	?
b. essential features and functions to be provided	1 2 3 4 5	1 2 3 4 5	1 2 3 4 5	1 2 3 4 5	?

25. Please indicate who has (or shares) decision responsibility for *day-to-day IS operations* that support *your business unit.*

	Corporate		Business Unit		Do Not Know
	corporate IS management	other corporate management	business unit IS management	other business unit management	
a. setting service delivery priorities when unforseen problems reduce planned service capacities in your business unit	1 2 3 4 5	1 2 3 4 5	1 2 3 4 5	1 2 3 4 5	?
b. overriding standard procedures when special IS service needs arise in your business unit	1 2 3 4 5	1 2 3 4 5	1 2 3 4 5	1 2 3 4 5	?
c. evaluating the quality of IS services in your business unit	1 2 3 4 5	1 2 3 4 5	1 2 3 4 5	1 2 3 4 5	?

Thank you for your cooperation in completing this questionaire. Your willingness to participate will help ensure the success of our project. Your firm will receive a summary of the study's results.